BrightRED Study Guide

CfE **HIGHER**

COMPUTING SCIENCE

Alan Williams

BrightRED
PUBLISHING

First published in 2014 by:
Bright Red Publishing Ltd
1 Torphichen Street
Edinburgh
EH3 8HX

Reprinted 2015

A CIP record for this book is available from the British Library.

ISBN 978-1-906736-60-6

With thanks to:
PDQ Digital Media Solutions Ltd, Bungay (layout), Ivor Normand (editorial).
Cover design and series book design by Caleb Rutherford – e i d e t i c.

Acknowledgements
Every effort has been made to seek all copyright-holders. If any have been overlooked, then Bright Red Publishing will be delighted to make the necessary arrangements.

Permission has been sought from all relevant copyright holders and Bright Red Publishing are grateful for the use of the following:

HultonArchive/iStock.com (page 6); ChristopherDodge/iStock.com (page 7); TatyanaGl/iStock.com (page 8); Adisa/Shutterstock.com (page 9); vierdrie/freeimages.com (page 10); Matthew Egginton/Shutterstock.com (page 12); Jeka/Shutterstock.com (page 13); wavebreakmedia/Shutterstock.com (page 15); wavebreakmedia/Shutterstock.com (page 15); racorn/Shutterstock.com (page 17); ADDRicky/iStock.com (page 17); Andrey_Popov/Shutterstock.com (page 23); Rawpixel/iStock.com (page 24); 4774344sean/iStock.com (page 25); 18percentgrey/Shutterstock.com (page 26); Images_of_Money (CC BY 2.0)[1] (page 29); Lilyana Vynogradova/Shutterstock.com (page 30); SMADE|MEDIA (CC BY 2.0)[1] (page 31); Bill Bradford (CC BY 2.0)[1] (page 33); Cover of Cake Craft & Decoration Magazine © Anglo American Media Ltd (page 36); cstrom/Creative Commons (CC BY-SA 2.0)[2] (page 36); Senior Airman Joshua Strang (public domain) (page 37); thiagofest/freeimages.com (page 39); Vasaleks/Shutterstock.com (page 39); Caleb Rutherford (page 40); Caleb Rutherford (page 41); (Mick Baker) rooster (CC BY-ND 2.0)[3] (page 42); rolve/freeimages.com (page 43); U.S. Army Environmental Command (CC BY 2.0)[1] (page 45); Tatiana Popova/Shutterstock.com (page 46); wavebreakmedia/Shutterstock.com (page 46); monkeybusinessimages/iStock.com (page 47); lonniehb/freeimages.com (page 48); QUEEN YUNA (CC BY-ND 2.0)[3] (page 49); ChevronZ (CC BY-SA 3.0)[1] (page 50); Sgt. Denise Serrano (public domain) (page 51); Caleb Rutherford (page 56); CaptainIFR/iStock.com (page 56); Caleb Rutherford (page 59); Ambrozjo/freeimages.com (page 60); Ebaychatter0 (CC BY-SA 3.0)[1] (page 61); adolf34/iStock.com (page 61); James Drury (CC BY 2.0)[1] (page 62); pipp/freeimages.com (page 63); pipp/freeimages.com (page 63); Caleb Rutherford (page 65); Windows 8 Release Preview Start Screen used with permission from Microsoft (page 65); jgroup/iStock.com (page 67); vierdrie/freeimages.com (page 67); brokenarts/freeimages.com (page 68); Caleb Rutherford (page 68); elementa1/freeimages.com (page 68); Pakmor/Shutterstock.com (page 69); Caleb Rutherford (page 70); foxumon/freeimages.com (page 70); inya/freeimages.com (page 70); hjalmeida/iStock.com (page 72); Caleb Rutherford & DragonTash/freeimages.com (page 73); Helga Esteb/Shutterstock.com (page 73); Chase Elliott Clark (CC BY 2.0)[1] (page 74); TaxRebate.org.uk (CC BY 2.0)[1] (page 75); Caleb Rutherford (page 76); kilukilu/iStock.com (page 77); Garsya/Shitterstock.com (page 78); wernerimages/iStock.com (page 79); wernerimages/iStock.com (page 79); Filip Krstic/Shutterstock.com (page 80); Ridofranz/iStock.com (page 81); Caleb Rutherford (page 82); **RCB**(CC BY 2.0)[1] (page 82); violetkaipa/iStock.com (page 83); koya79/iStock.com (page 84); Sagadogo/iStock.com (page 85); gokoroko/freeimages.com (page 86); imtnbike (CC BY 2.0)[1] (page 88); Douglas Woods (CC BY 2.0)[1] (page 88); Christian Cable (CC BY 2.0)[1] (page 89); David Shankbone (CC BY 3.0)[4] (page 89); rawartistsmedia (CC BY-ND 2.0)[3] (page 90); NTNU Trondheim (CC BY-SA 2.0)[2] (page 91); NTNU Trondheim (CC BY-SA 2.0)[2] (page 91); rawartistsmedia (CC BY-ND 2.0)[3] (page 91); David Robert Bliwas (CC BY 2.0)[1] (page 91); rawartistsmedia (CC BY-ND 2.0)[3] (page 91); style-photographs/iStock.com (page 92); Qwasyx/iStock.com (page 95).

(CC BY 2.0)[1]   http://creativecommons.org/licenses/by/2.0/
(CC BY-SA 2.0)[2] http://creativecommons.org/licenses/by-sa/2.0/
(CC BY-ND 2.0)[3] http://creativecommons.org/licenses/by-nd/2.0/
(CC BY 3.0)[4]   http://creativecommons.org/licenses/by-sa/3.0/

Printed and bound in the UK by Latimer Trend & Company Ltd.

CONTENTS

HIGHER COURSE

SYLLABUS AND ASSESSMENT

INTRODUCTION

The main purpose of this book is to improve your chances of success in the Higher Computing Science course. The knowledge required for the exam and unit assessments is provided clearly and concisely. The book is intended not to cover wider issues beyond the syllabus but to present you with revision materials in a summarised version that targets the requirements of the exam. Regularly studying this book will go a long way towards your success in this course.

SYLLABUS

This course is made up of three units:

1 Software Design and Development
2 Information System Design and Development
3 Value-added Unit

The first two units are mandatory and provide the content on which the course assessment is based.
An outline of the contents of each unit is given in the tables below.

Software Design and Development		
Languages and environments	Low-level and high-level languages Procedural languages	Declarative languages Object-oriented languages
Data types and structures	String Numeric (Integer and Real) variables Boolean variables	One-dimensional (1-D) arrays Records
Computational constructs	Subprograms and user-defined functions Parameter passing (value and reference, formal and actual)	Scope, local and global variables Sequential files (open/create, read, write, close, delete)
Testing	Constructing a test plan incorporating normal, extreme and exceptional testing Syntax, execution and logic errors Dry runs, trace tables (tools), breakpoints	
Algorithm specification	Input validation Linear search	Find minimum and maximum Count occurrences
Design notations	Structure diagram Pseudocode	Wire-framing
Phases of the development process	Analysis, design, implementation, testing, documentation, evaluation, maintenance	
Development methodologies	Top-down/stepwise refinement Rapid application development	Agile methodologies
Low-level operations	Virtual machines Emulators Mobile devices	Binary representation of integers, real numbers, characters, graphics (bit-mapped and vector), video, sound, instructions (machine code)
Computer architecture	Processor(s), memory, cache, buses, interfaces	
Contemporary developments	Trends in the development of: software development languages, software development environments, intelligent systems, online systems	

Information System Design and Development		
Structures and links	Database structures: • Relational, web-based • Tables, relationships, interface, scripting • Complex database operations (queries, forms, reports) • Data dictionary	Web-page structure: • Head, title, body, metadata • Stylesheets, CSS • Dynamic web page, database-driven website • Interactive web page, multimedia application • Multi-level navigation
User interface	Usability: fit for purpose, efficient, robust, maintainable	Accessibility Optimisation

contd

Media types	Compression: lossy and lossless Compression techniques, applied to sound, graphic and video data files	
Coding	Client-side scripting	Server-side scripting
Testing	Beta testing Compatibility issues (including memory and storage requirements, OS compatibility)	Usability
Purpose, features, functionality, users	Detailed descriptions of purpose Users	Human: expert, novice, age-range Machine: search engines (crawlers and bots)
Technical implementation (requirements)	Hardware considerations: • Input and output devices • Processor type, number and speed (Hz) • Memory (RAM, ROM, cache) • Device type (including supercomputer, desktop, laptop, tablet, smartphone)	Software considerations: • Operating systems • Licensing • Proprietary versus open source • Portability • Description and exemplification of current trends in operating system design
Technical implementation (storage)	Storage devices: • Built-in, external, portable • Magnetic, optical • Solid-state • Capacity, speed • Rewritable, read-only	• Interface type and speed • Distributed and offline storage • Backup systems and strategy • Description and exemplification of current trends in storage systems
Technical implementation (networking/connectivity)	Cloud systems and server provision: • Public, private, hybrid • Cloud-based services	• Web hosting • Description and exemplification of current trends in networking and connectivity
Security risks	Spyware, phishing, keylogging Online fraud, identity theft	DOS (Denial of Service) attacks
Security precautions	Encryption Digital certificates and signatures	Server-side validation of online form data Biometrics in industry
Legal implications	Computer Misuse Act Copyright, Designs and Patents Act (plagiarism)	Communication Acts Regulation of Investigatory Powers Act
Environmental implications	Lifetime carbon footprint (manufacture, use, disposal)	Environmental benefits
Economic and social impact	Economic: competitive advantage, global marketplace, business costs, maintainability, scalability	Social: censorship and freedom of speech, privacy and encryption, global citizenship, online communities

ASSESSMENT

The course assessment consists of an examination and a practical assignment. More details on the structure of these components are given at the end of this book.

Component 1   Exam paper: 90 marks
Component 2   Assignment: 60 marks
Total: 150 marks.

Grades

You will be given an overall grade (A–D) calculated from the total of the two marks. A brief description of the standard required to achieve each grade is given below.

Grades are awarded for levels of performance in the skills, knowledge and understanding of the course, as follows: A: consistently high; B: fairly high; C: successful; D: unsatisfactory.

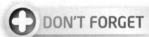 DON'T FORGET

In addition to your performance in the course assessment, you must also have passed the unit assessments to gain your grade award for this course. The unit assessments are assessed as a pass or fail, and do not determine your overall grade; but you must pass them to complete the course.

 THINGS TO DO AND THINK ABOUT

Be aware of the marks allocated to the assessments for this course. Don't spend too much time on a component worth fewer marks at the expense of losing lots of marks in a more important component. There is a marking scheme for both the course assignment and the exam.

LANGUAGES AND ENVIRONMENTS 1

LOW-LEVEL AND HIGH-LEVEL LANGUAGES

Early computer programs were written in low-level binary code. Since then, hundreds of high-level programming languages have been developed to cater for the wide diversity of application areas in which they are applied. The requirements of a programming language being used to develop an artificial-intelligence program are very different from the requirements for a program being developed to process scientific data.

Low-level Languages (Machine Code and Assembly Language)

Before the existence of high-level programming languages, computers were programmed one instruction at a time using machine code, which is a program consisting of binary codes. This was an extremely time-consuming task, with lots of errors being created in the process.

Software development at this time was very expensive, and programs were mainly used to perform arithmetic calculations, since they were much faster and accurate than a human. This led to the development of assembly languages that made programming easier but still required specialist technical ability.

Assembly-language programs replaced binary codes with very short text codes, but the instructions still have a one-to-one correspondence with the equivalent machine-code program. Assembly languages use an assembler to translate the code into machine code before it is executed.

Assembly language can be considered as an intermediate step between machine code and high-level languages.

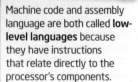

DON'T FORGET

Machine code and assembly language are both called **low-level languages** because they have instructions that relate directly to the processor's components.

Example: Machine code

```
10111001 00110010 01010001
01000011 00111111 10101011
11111110 11110000 11000010
10001100 00000111 11001010
00110010 11111110 01010111
11100011 00001010 01010011
etc.
```

Example: Assembly-language code

```
Add N1, N2
Add N3, N4
Mov N1, N5
Mov N3, N6
Sub N5, N6
Prt N5
etc.
```

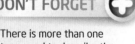

DON'T FORGET

There is more than one term used to describe the selection and repetition control constructs. **Selection** is sometimes referred to as **branching**, since the program branches to one or more instructions if a condition is true. **Repetition** is sometimes referred to as **iteration** or **looping**.

High-level Languages

As computers became more and more widespread in the 1960s and 1970s, people wanted to use computers to solve larger and more complex problems in a variety of application areas. Low-level languages were far too time-consuming and error-prone to solve such complex problems. As a result, high-level programming languages began to appear in the mid-1950s.

High-level-language programs are much easier to write and to debug (find and solve errors in) than low-level-language programs, for the following reasons:

- They use everyday English command words.

- They use data types such as Integer, Real, String and Boolean.

- They use data structures such as arrays.

- Complex arithmetical calculations can be performed in one instruction using $+, -, *, /, \char94$ (e.g. Let Hypotenuse = Sqr(Side1 $\char94$ 2 + Side2 $\char94$ 2).

contd

- Logical operations such as +, -, * , /, AND, OR, NOT, etc.

- One high-level-language instruction translates into many machine-code instructions.

- The program can be broken down into subprograms (procedures and functions) with parameters to pass data in and out of the subroutines.

- They have inbuilt functions to perform mathematical and textual processing of data (Left(), Format(), Sin() and so on).

- Sequencing, selection and repetition control constructs.

Example: High-level-language code

```
Let Age = Inputbox("Please enter your age.")
If Age < 18 Then
    Picture1.Print "Please leave now."
End If
etc.
```

Some programs are still created in a low-level language in situations where the speed of execution is critical. This is because software written in a low-level language communicates directly with the processor and not indirectly through a translator, which produces less efficient code.

DON'T FORGET

The computer only understands instructions in its own programming language. Therefore, all high-level-language programs have to be translated into machine code to be executed.

PROCEDURAL LANGUAGES

A procedural language follows a pre-defined and well-organised set of subprograms in a sequence of steps to solve a problem. A program written in a procedural language has a clear start and end to the program. The set of instructions which the program follows to solve a problem is called an algorithm.

Data is stored in data structures such as **arrays**, and then it is processed using procedures and functions that are separate from the data. This methodology groups instructions into subprograms (procedures and functions), which use parameters to pass data in and out.

In languages such as C, Python and Java, the program is written in terms of subprograms which can access global variables from anywhere in a program. This introduces the possibility of error by accidentally changing a global variable. Also, maintaining programs involves tracking through the entire program to see if changing a global variable has any effect on each subroutine.

VIDEO LINK

Watch a video describing the differences between low-level and high-level programming at www. brightredbooks.net

ONLINE

Investigate procedural languages further by entering the keywords 'Wikipedia' and 'procedural' and 'language' into a search engine.

 ## THINGS TO DO AND THINK ABOUT

Programming languages can be classified into groups according to their structure and characteristics. Consider what classification of languages you have used in your practical work at school or at college. You might have used Python, Visual Basic, JavaScript and so on.

ONLINE TEST

How well have you learned about languages and environments? Take the test at www. brightredbooks.net

LANGUAGES AND ENVIRONMENTS 2

DECLARATIVE LANGUAGES

A declarative language allows the programmer to create a knowledge base which contains facts and rules about a problem. A query is then used to interrogate the knowledge base and to draw conclusions.

These types of language are very good at logic but are not good at programs requiring calculations, since they have limited support for numeric data types. Prolog is an example of a declarative language.

Declarative languages are used to develop expert systems in areas such as medical diagnosis and aircraft repair.

Shown below is an example of the rules and facts used by an expert system for determining family relationships.

Facts:
parent(william, rosie)   means that William is a parent of Rosie.
parent(connie, alan)   means that Connie is a parent of Alan.
female(rosie)   means that Rosie is a female
male(william)   means that William is a male.

Rules:
father(X, Y) :-parent(X, Y),male(X)   means that X is a father of Y if X is a parent of Y and X s a male.

A query such as father(X, rosie) would provide the result X=william.

Recursion

A form of looping known as **recursion** is found in declarative languages.
Recursion is the process of a procedure calling itself.
The procedure shown below adds 7% to an account balance every time it is called up.

```
TO AddInterest
SET Balance TO Balance * 1.07
AddInterest
END SUB
```

The procedure shown here would repeat itself to infinity, so a mechanism has to be put in place to stop the procedure from calling itself.

```
SET Counter TO 0
TO AddInterest
SET Counter TO Counter + 1
SET Balance TO Balance * 1.07
AddInterest
IF Counter = 10 THEN STOP
End Sub
```

The variable counter is set to 0 before the procedure is called, and is then incremented by 1 each time the procedure calls itself. The recursion loop ends when the counter reaches 10.

OBJECT-ORIENTED LANGUAGES

In procedural languages, the program is written in terms of subprograms which can access global variables from anywhere in a program. This introduces the possibility of error by accidentally changing a global variable. Also, maintaining programs involves tracking through the entire program to see if changing a global variable has any effect on each subroutine.

Object-oriented programming was introduced to overcome this problem by using a model centred around objects, where each object encapsulates both the data and the code that manipulates the data.

Objects

The real world consists of objects: a car, a house, a student and so on. Each of these objects has data (attributes) and operations (methods) that can be applied to them.

Example:

For example, a ListBox object can have attributes and methods as shown:

Setting attributes
List1.BackColor = RGB(255, 0, 0)   Sets the back colour of the ListBox to red.
List1.Height = 5000   Sets the height of the ListBox to 5,000 pixels.

Applying methods
List1.AddItem "Dopey"   Adds the item 'Dopey' to the ListBox.
List1.Clear   Clears the contents of the ListBox.

This table shows some data and operations for a car object:

Data (attributes)	Operations (methods)
Manufacturer, engine size, top speed etc.	Accelerating, braking, refuelling etc.

Encapsulation

Data and operations are not separate but are bound together within an object. This improves module independence, since data cannot be changed within objects by other objects.

Classes

A class is a collection of objects that have a set of common characteristics.

For example, a car is just one of many makes of car. Because of this, a class can be created to accommodate all makes of car.

Inheritance

This is the process by which a subclass or object which is created from a main class automatically acquires all the characteristics of the main class.

By use of inheritance, an object need only define those qualities that make it unique within its class, since it can inherit its general characteristics from its main class.

If an error is corrected in the main class, it is automatically fixed in all derived subclasses and objects.

This can be significant in a large project, which could contain dozens of objects derived from a class.

 THINGS TO DO AND THINK ABOUT

You have probably used the Scratch programming language for computer-games development. Scratch is essentially an object-oriented programming language in data (costumes); and operations (code) are encapsulated in the sprite objects.

 ONLINE

Use a search engine to find definitions of the terms 'object', 'encapsulation', 'class', 'inheritance' and 'polymorphism'. Use multiple keywords such as 'inheritance object oriented language'.

ONLINE

You can read more about procedural and object-oriented programming at www.brightredbooks.net

 ONLINE

Enter 'procedural vs object-oriented' into a search engine for a detailed comparison of these types of programming languages.

 ONLINE TEST

How well have you learned about languages and environments? Take the test at www.brightredbooks.net

DATA TYPES AND STRUCTURES

INTRODUCTION

Programs need to be able to store text, whole numbers, decimal numbers and so on. Data types are used to store different types of data within a program. In this course, you need to know about String, Integer, Real and Boolean data types.

Each data type is stored differently in main memory. For example, a programming language might store an **integer** in a 32-bit two's complement notation, while a **real** data type is stored as a floating-point number with a 32-bit mantissa and a 16-bit exponent. Declaring a variable as a specific data type allows the translator to allocate memory to store the program's variable. It also restricts the range of operations which can be performed on any given type and helps the programmer to avoid making silly mistakes such as trying to multiply two letters together.

STRING

A **string** data type is used to store an item of text and a sequence of characters.

This data type would be used to store a colour, the name of a pet, a question in a quiz and so on.
String data is enclosed in quotation marks to let the program know that it is not a number but an item of text.
For example, "Paris", "hockey", "rose petal", "What is the height of King Kong?" etc. should be stored in a **string** data type.

CHAR

Some languages have a **char** data type, which is used to store a single character.
This data type could be used to store "M" or "F" for the sex of a person.
For example, "T", "F", "H" or "L" should be stored in a **char** data type.

INTEGER

An **integer** data type is used to store positive and negative whole numbers, and zero.
This data type would be used to store the score when throwing a die, the number of students in a school, winning lottery numbers and so on.
For example, 7, 80, –20, 0, –57, 702 should be stored in an **integer** data type.

REAL

A **real** data type is used to store positive and negative decimal or fractional numbers.
This data type can be used to store the height of a girl in metres, the winning time for a 100 metres race, the weight in kg of a melon and so on.
For example, 2·5, 3·14, –6·57, 25·0, –400·783 should be stored in a **real** data type.

DON'T FORGET

The data type Boolean should have a capital letter, because it is named after the British mathematician George Boole, who helped to establish modern algebra of logic.

BOOLEAN VARIABLES

A **Boolean variable** is used to store only two values: True and False.
This data type would be used to store the answer to a 'true or false?' question, whether someone is married or not, whether a number entered into a program is valid or not, and so on.

	True	False
Five spiders have more legs than seven wasps?	☐	☐

ONE-DIMENSIONAL (1-D) ARRAYS

Many programs require to store and manipulate not just one item of data but a list of related data items. An array is used to store a group of data where the data is all of the same data type.

For example, an array could be used to store 20 marks for students in an exam, the names of 60 contacts on a mobile phone, the answer to 40 multiple-choice exam questions, and so on.

Each element of the array is identified by using the array name with an index number in brackets (sometimes called the subscript) of the array.

When an array is declared, its size (or dimension) is stated.

The diagram below represents an array called 'Dwarfs', which stores 7 strings. This array would be declared with a statement of the form 'Dim Dwarfs(6) as String'. The '6' in brackets indicates that the highest index in the array is to be 6. This means that this array will store 7 items of data, since the first index is zero.

Dwarfs	(0)	(1)	(2)	(3)	(4)	(5)	(6)
	Dopey	Bashful	Sneezy	Sleepy	Happy	Grumpy	Doc

An element of the 'Dwarfs' array can be referred to using the array name with the subscript in index.

Example:

For example: Dwarfs(4) = "Happy"

This statement assigns the string "Happy" to variable number 5 of the array called 'Dwarfs'.

Dwarfs	(0)	(1)	(2)	(3)	(4)	(5)	(6)
					Happy		

Record Data Type

A record data type is a data structure which can store variables of different data types in fields.

It provides a means of collecting together a set of different data types into one named structure.

When performing operations such as sorting, a record data structure is preferable to using a number of parallel 1-D arrays, where there is no built-in link between the arrays, and the array indices may become unsynchronised. All the data in the fields of a record are moved together as a unit.

For example, the definition shown below creates a record data type called Students using a Type statement.

```
Type Student
      FirstName As String
      SurName As String
      Sex As Char
      Height As Single
      Exam As Integer
End Type
```

An array of the Student data type can then be declared to store a group of records. Each record is identified by an index just like any array.

For example, Dim Students(59) As Student

THINGS TO DO AND THINK ABOUT

Programming languages have a variety of data types. When you are writing your own programs in your practical work, think carefully about the variables required to store your program's data, and declare them with the correct data type.

 ONLINE

Follow the 'Data Types and Structures' link at www.brightredbooks.net and enter the word 'array' into the search box. The site has information on how to declare arrays, enter data into arrays and process the data in an array.

 **DON'T FORGET**

In your programming tasks, you should always use an array to store a list of items. The program will be much more efficient than if you store each item in a separate variable.

 VIDEO LINK

See examples of different data types at www.brightredbooks.net

 ONLINE TEST

Test yourself on this topic online at www.brightredbooks.net

COMPUTATIONAL CONSTRUCTS 1

VARIABLES

The data used by a program is stored in main-memory storage locations. A variable is the name that the program uses to identify the location that is storing an item of data. Using meaningful names for variables, such as Score1 and Length, makes the program more readable.

Declaring Variables

Most programming languages require variables to be declared before they are used.

Declaring variables has several advantages:

1 The translator can set aside areas of main memory to hold the data.
2 The program is more readable, since variables do not suddenly appear in instructions without an advance warning to the programmer.
3 When a variable is declared, its data type is also declared, which tells the translator how to represent the data in memory.

SCOPE OF VARIABLES

The aim in good programming is to limit the scope of program variables as far as possible. This means that the effect of any changes to the variable during modifications to the program need only be traced through a part of the program and not the whole program. This makes program maintenance much easier.

Local Variables

A local variable only exists within the subprogram (procedure or function) in which it is declared.

It can only be changed within that subprogram and will not be recognised by any other subprogram.

Global Variables

A global variable is recognised by all the subprograms within the program. It can be changed by any subprogram in the program.

The aim is to minimise the number of global variables, since any change to a global variable in one subprogram must be traced through every other subprogram to see how they are affected. This is not a significant problem in a small program but has enormous consequences in large-scale commercial programs.

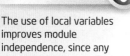

DON'T FORGET

The use of local variables improves module independence, since any changes to the module (subprogram) only affect the module in which the changes are made and not the rest of the program.

VIDEO LINK

For more on local and global variables, visit www. brightredbooks.net

DON'T FORGET

You only need to know about sequential files for this course. Most programming languages allow the creation and manipulation of direct-access files; but you can ignore them for your course assessments.

SEQUENTIAL FILES

Programs require to access and manipulate files saved on a backing storage device.

A sequential file stores items of data items one after another and is terminated with an end-of-file (EOF) marker.

Example:

The data in this table could be stored in a sequential file as shown:

Name	Age	Birthday
Alan Tucker	15	12 Jun
Suzie Forfar	14	24 Dec
Sam Dastardly	17	31 Mar
...	...	...

Sequential file:

Alan Tucker	15	12 Jun	Suzie Forfar	14	24 Dec	Sam Dastardly	...	EOF

FILE OPERATIONS

There are several file-handling operations that allow files to be created, accessed and manipulated. These operations include open/create, read, write, close, delete. Different programming languages will have different syntax for file operations, but the pseudocode used in the following examples indicates the essential principles.

Open/Create

A file must be opened before input and output operations can be performed on it. This allows the operating system to make memory available to store the file.

This is achieved with a command to open the file, followed by the filename.

If the file doesn't exist, then it is created when a file is opened for writing.

Example:
```
OPEN Filename
CREATE Filename
```

Close

After it has been opened and read or written to, a file must be closed so that the computer's operating system can make the memory available for other data. This is achieved with a command to close the file, followed by the filename.

Example:
```
CLOSE Filename
```

Read

'Read' is the operation where items of data in a file are input into main memory. The example below reads a file into an array with 10 elements.

Example:
```
OPEN Filename
FOR Count FROM 0 TO 9 DO
    RECEIVE Array(Count) FROM Filename
END FOR
CLOSE Filename
```

Write

'Write' is the operation where items of data in main memory are output to a file. The example below writes the items in an array with 20 elements to a file.

Example:
```
OPEN Filename
FOR Count FROM 0 TO 19 DO
    SEND Array(Count) TO Filename
END FOR
CLOSE Filename
```

Delete

'Delete' is the process of permanently removing a file from the backing storage device.

Example:
```
DELETE Filename
```

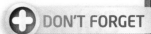

DON'T FORGET

File operations manage the files held in backing storage, but the data stored in an array is manipulated in main memory.

ONLINE TEST

Head to www. brightredbooks.net and take the test on computational constructs.

 THINGS TO DO AND THINK ABOUT

The programming language that you use for your practical work will have file-handling operations. Use the language's online help to investigate these operations.

COMPUTATIONAL CONSTRUCTS 2

SUBPROGRAMS

Programs are modularised by breaking them down into subprograms (procedures and functions), which makes the program easier to manage and understand.

The examples used for illustration in this spread are written in the Visual Basic programming language, but the same principles apply to other languages.

Procedures

A procedure produces an effect, e.g. sorting a list of marks, displaying a menu, and so on.

Shown below is the definition of a procedure which calculates the perimeter and area of a rectangle and displays the results.

```
Sub RectangleFacts(Length, Breadth)
'This procedure finds the perimeter and area of a rectangle and displays the results
Dim Perimeter As Single
Dim Area As Single
Let Perimeter = 2 * (Length + Breadth)
Let Area = Length * Breadth
Picture1.Print "The perimeter of the rectangle is " & Perimeter
Picture1.Print "The area of the rectangle is " & Area
End Sub
```

The procedure is then used in a program with statements such as:
'Call RectangleFacts(L, B)'; 'Call RectangleFacts(3, 8)' and so on.

Functions

A function returns a single value, e.g. returning the mode of an array of numbers, returning the number of vowels in a string, and so on.

Shown below is the definition of a function to return the maximum value in an integer array.

```
Function Max(Scores() As Integer) As Integer
'This function returns the highest value in an array of integers.
Dim Max As Integer
Let Max = Scores(0)
For i = 1 To 9
    If Scores(i) > Max Then
        Let Max = Scores(i)
    End If
Next i
End Function
```

The function is then used in the program with statements such as:
Let Highest = Max(Numbers())
Picture1.Print "The best mark was " & Max(Marks())

Programming languages usually have many inbuilt functions such as Sin(), SQR(), Left() to save the programmer from writing the code from scratch.

DON'T FORGET

A user-defined function is a function that has been written and saved by a programmer to be used over and over again in the future. An inbuilt function is a function that is part of the programming language to make it more efficient for the programmer to develop code.

PARAMETERS

A **parameter** is a variable or value that is passed into and/or out of a subprogram. There are two types of parameters:

- The **formal** parameters are used in the subprogram definition.
- The **actual** parameters are passed into the subprogram when it is called from another part of the program.

contd

Arguments

The term **argument** is sometimes used to refer to the actual value (also known as the actual parameter) passed to a subprogram when it is used.

PASSING PARAMETERS BY REFERENCE AND BY VALUE

There are two methods of passing parameters:

- Passing parameters by **reference** is used when the value being passed in is to be updated and passed back out again. (The variable itself is passed into the subprogram so that any changes to the variable will change the variable.)

- Passing parameters by **value** is used when a value is passed in to a subprogram but does not require to be passed out. (The subprogram makes a copy of the variable so that any changes to the copy of the variable will not change the variable.)

Example:

The program shown below asks for the length and breadth of a rectangle and then calculates the area and displays the result.

Procedure declaration: *Length + Breadth* are **formal** parameters

```
Dim L As Integer
Dim B As Integer

Sub GetSides(ByRef Length As Integer, ByRef Breadth As Integer)
'Get the length and breadth of the rectangle
Let Length = InputBox("Please enter the length of the rectangle.")
Let Breadth = InputBox("Please enter the breadth of the rectangle.")
End Sub
Function Area(ByVal Length As Integer, ByVal Breadth As Integer) As Integer
'Calculate the area of the rectangle
Let Area = Length * Breadth
End Function
Private Sub Command1_Click()
Call GetSides(L, B)
End Sub
Private Sub Command2_Click()
Picture1.Print "The area of the rectangle is " & Area(L, B)
End Sub
```

Procedure call: *L + B* are **actual** parameters

Function declaration: *Length + Breadth* are **formal** parameters

Function call: *L + B* are **actual** parameters

MODULE LIBRARIES

A module library is a collection of pre-written subprograms that are available to a programmer to speed up the software-development process.

Advantages of Module Libraries

1 Time is saved in writing the same programming code over and over again.
2 The module will be tried and tested, and therefore should be free from errors.
3 Complex and difficult programming algorithms can be evoked simply by calling an existing module written by an expert programmer.

The documentation for a module in a module library will include items such as:
1 a description of the function of the module
2 the parameters that are passed in and out of the module and their data types
3 the programming language in which it is written.

THINGS TO DO AND THINK ABOUT

In your practical programming tasks, always use a function and not a procedure to return a single value such as an average or a maximum.

TESTING

CONSTRUCTING A TEST PLAN

Before a program is tested, a test plan should be constructed. This is a document that describes the approach and test data that is to be used to test the program. It is impossible to test a large program with the huge amount of possible permutations of input data. However, test data should be chosen to test that the software can cope with as many cases as possible, as far as time and expense allows.

A mixture of normal, extreme and exceptional data should be used to test the software thoroughly. This is known as comprehensive testing, since the selection of test data is wide-ranging.

Normal Data

One set of test data should be chosen to test that the software gives correct results for commonplace data without any unusual or extreme data.

Extreme Data

One set of test data should be chosen to see if the software can handle data on the edge or limits.

Exceptional Data

One set of test data should be chosen for extreme cases in order to test the robustness of the software.

Example:

A program enters 7 exam marks as a percentage. The program then displays the number of marks in each grade (Fail 0...49, C 50...59, B 60...69, A 70...100).

The following sets of data would cover a good range of cases:
Normal test data   Marks 67, 34, 78, 56, 63, 40, 51
Extreme data   Marks 50, 100, 0, 60, 70, 49, 69
Exceptional data   Marks 144, –13, 50·5, 66A, 7000000, A, Polly

SYNTAX, EXECUTION AND LOGIC ERRORS

Syntax Error

These are mistakes in the grammar of the programming language. They are reported by the translator, since they are breaking the rules of the language and can't be translated.

Here are some examples of syntax errors:
1   Misspellings of language keywords: e.g. Prnt, Nexy I and so on
2   Missing inverted commas: e.g. Picture1.Print "Hello
3   A For...Next loop with a For but no Next.

Execution Error

These are errors that are not detected by the translator but are discovered when the program is run.

A common execution error occurs when the program is instructed to divide by zero, which generates an error – and the program will crash. Another example is when a program attempts to read data from a file on disc, and the disc is not present in the disc drive. Good software should have error-trapping techniques to avoid these errors.

Execution errors are also known as run-time errors, since they are errors that prevent the instruction from being run.

contd

Logical Error

A program can translate error-free and have no run-time errors but still not give correct results, because of error in the logic of the instructions – for example, writing code to add two numbers instead of multiplying them, or subtracting two numbers the wrong way round.

DRY RUNS, TRACE TABLES, BREAKPOINTS

Dry Run

This technique involves stepping through the program instructions and manually working out on paper how the program variables are updated. This involves updating the value of variables, usually in a table, after the execution of each instruction to check that the correct logical steps are being followed by the program code.

Trace Table

A trace is used by a programmer to manually step through the program line by line while watching how variables are updated in a trace table after each instruction has been executed.

Example:

The trace table below shows how the values of the variables AnnualPay, QuarterlyBonus and the condition Count > 3 are updated when the following code is stepped through one line at a time.

```
SET AnnualPay TO 35000
SET QuarterlyBonus TO 400
SET Count TO 0
REPEAT
    SET AnnualPay TO AnnualPay + QuarterlyBonus
    SET Count TO Count + 1
UNTIL Count > 3
```

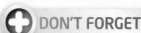
 DON'T FORGET

A dry run can be used to locate logical errors in the program, but it will not find syntax errors. It can also help to identify run-time errors such as dividing by zero.

AnnualPay	QuarterlyBonus	Count	Count > 3
35000			
	400		
		0	
35400			
		1	
			False
35800			
		2	
			False
36200			
		3	
			False
36600			
		4	
			True

Breakpoint

A breakpoint is set as a marker alongside an instruction in the program. When the program reaches the breakpoint, program execution is suspended. The contents of the variables in the program can then be examined, typically by hovering over a variable in the code with the mouse pointer; and a small text box displays the value of the variable.

ONLINE

Follow the link at www.brightredbooks.net to find several videos showing how to use breakpoints to help in debugging a program.

 ONLINE TEST

Test yourself on this topic online at www.brightredbooks.net

 ## THINGS TO DO AND THINK ABOUT

Explore the software-development tools provided by the programming language that you use. Trace tables and breakpoints are provided with most programming languages.

ALGORITHM SPECIFICATION

INTRODUCTION

Standard algorithms such as sorting a list, finding a maximum value, counting the numbers of passes in an exam, and so on, appear in programs over and over again.

This course covers five standard algorithms that are commonly used in programs:

1 Input validation
2 Linear search
3 Finding maximum
4 Finding minimum
5 Counting occurrences.

INPUT VALIDATION

Input validation involves avoiding input errors by repeatedly asking for data to be entered until it is an acceptable value.

Example:

This example enters and validates a percentage mark in the range 0 to 100.

```
1   REPEAT
2      RECEIVE Mark FROM KEYBOARD
3      IF Mark < 0 OR Mark > 100 THEN
4         SEND ["Not possible. Try again!"] TO DISPLAY
5      END IF
6   UNTIL Mark > = 0 AND Mark <= 100
```

LINEAR SEARCH

This algorithm searches for a value at the first item in a list and continues searching through each item of the list in turn.

Example:

This example searches the entire list from start to finish and stops only when the end of the list is reached.

```
1   SET Position TO 0
2   RECEIVE SearchValue FROM KEYBOARD
3   REPEAT
4      IF Item(Position) = SearchValue THEN
5         SEND [SearchValue] TO DISPLAY
6      END IF
7      SET Position TO Position + 1
8   UNTIL Position = No of items in list
```

This algorithm is not efficient, since it continues to search to the end of the list even if the search value has been found.

The following improved algorithm makes use of a condition that will stop the search once the search value has been found.

```
1    SET Found TO FALSE
2    SET Position TO 0
3    RECEIVE SearchValue FROM KEYBOARD
4    REPEAT
5       IF Item(Position) = SearchValue THEN
6          SET Found TO TRUE
7          SEND [SearchValue] TO DISPLAY
8       ELSE
9          SET Position TO Position + 1
10      END IF
11   UNTIL (Found = TRUE) OR (Position = No of items in list)
12   IF Found = FALSE THEN
13      SEND ["Message not found."] TO DISPLAY
14   END IF
```

FINDING MAXIMUM

This algorithm is used to find the maximum value in a list.

1 a max variable is set to the first item in the list
2 each item in the list in turn is compared to the max to see if it is bigger
3 every time the item in the list is bigger than the max, the max is updated to that item.

Example:

Finding the maximum in a list of items:

```
1   SET Position TO 0
2   SET Max TO Item(Position)
3   FOR Position FROM 1 TO No of items in list – 1 DO
4       IF Item(Position) > Max THEN
5           SET Max TO Item(Position)
6       END IF
7   END FOR
8   SEND ["The maximum value is ", Max] TO DISPLAY
```

ONLINE

The linear-search algorithm is a suitable algorithm for a short list. Another standard algorithm called a **binary search** is much more efficient at searching for a value in a long list. Use a search engine to research the binary-search algorithm.

FINDING MINIMUM

This algorithm is virtually identical to finding the maximum value, only each item in the list is compared to the min to see if it is smaller.

Example:

Finding the minimum in a list of items:

```
1   SET Position TO 0
2   SET Min TO Item(Position)
3   FOR Position FROM 1 TO No of items in list – 1 DO
4       IF Item(Position) < Min THEN
5           SET Min TO Item(Position)
6       END IF
7   END FOR
8   SEND ["The minimum value is ", Min] TO DISPLAY
```

DON'T FORGET

Although finding the maximum and finding the minimum are covered as two separate algorithms, they are almost identical.

ONLINE TEST

Take the test on algorithm specification at www.brightredbooks.net

COUNTING OCCURRENCES

This algorithm counts how often a value occurs in a list of items.

1 set a counter to zero
2 search a list for the occurrence of a search value
3 increment the counter by 1 each time the search value is found.

Example:

Counting occurrences of a search value in a list of items:

```
1   SET Count TO 0
2   RECEIVE SearchValue FROM KEYBOARD
3   FOR Position FROM 0 TO No of items in list – 1 DO
4       IF SearchValue = Item(position) THEN
5           SET Count TO Count + 1
6       END IF
7   END FOR
8   SEND [Count] TO DISPLAY
```

THINGS TO DO AND THINK ABOUT

The version of pseudocode shown in these examples used to be called 'Haggis', which you will have met in the National 5 course. This standardised pseudocode has been extended to take account of extra programming features that are required for the Higher course, such as file-handling operations, and functions and procedures.

DESIGN NOTATIONS

WIRE-FRAMING

A wireframe is used early in the development of software to provide a skeletal outline of the components of a program interface before detailing the specifics.

A wireframe uses basic boxes and lines to define the spaces on the page to indicate where interface elements such as command buttons, pull-down menus, text, images etc. will be placed before the actual content is created. Using a wireframe to design the program interface improves the clarity and consistency of the interface.

The example below shows a wireframe which indicates where images, text, navigation controls and command buttons are positioned. The details of the content of these elements of the program interface are not specified at this stage.

Example:

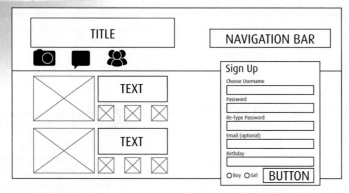

STRUCTURE DIAGRAM

The structure of the program is how it is divided up into subprograms and how they communicate with each other. The structure of a program is sometimes referred to as the program architecture.

Stepwise Refinement

This is the process of repeatedly breaking down larger, difficult problems step by step into smaller and smaller, easier-to-solve problems.

It is easier for a human being to solve a series of small problems than a large and difficult problem. 'Divide and conquer' is a well-known phrase to describe this process.

One advantage of this approach is that it also automatically gives a structure to the solution.

It also means that, once manageable parts have been identified in a large project, the analyst can then assign individual tasks to different teams of programmers.

There is also the possibility that there already exists a tried and tested subprogram to provide the code for a small part of the program – for example, a subprogram that sorts a list of data into order or calculates statistics on the items in an array. This can save time and costs in the development of the program.

Top-down Design

Stepwise refinement is sometimes called **top-down design**, for the obvious reason that you start the process at the top, with the problem as a whole, and work downwards in steps of refinement.

contd

Structure Diagram/Structure Chart

A structure diagram shows the hierarchy of the program components and how they are linked together.

It shows the decomposition of the program in a series of steps into smaller and smaller blocks.

The representation is hierarchical in that each level relates to a refinement of the level above.

Different symbols are used in a structure diagram as follows:

a module requiring further refinement

selection

repetition

a statement requiring no further refinement

Example:

A structure diagram representing the calculation of the average of a list of exam marks:

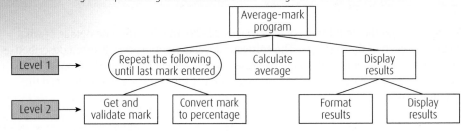

DON'T FORGET

A structure diagram is more than a picture of boxes showing the parts of a program. It is a common mistake **not** to describe it as a hierarchy where each level is a refinement of the level above.

PSEUDOCODE

Pseudocode is used at the design stage to give the detailed logic of the program code.

The prefix 'pseudo-' means 'not actual but having the appearance of'. This points to what pseudocode is, in that it is not actual program instructions, but it has the same logic and appearance as program code. It lies somewhere between programming code and natural language.

Three features of pseudocode are:

1   It describes the detailed logic of a program without having to bother about the details of how it is going to be implemented in the chosen programming language.

2   It shows the control constructs of the algorithm, i.e. looping, branching and so on.

3   It shows the stepwise refinement of the problem in levels of decomposition.

```
Level 1
1   Get Mark
2   Find Grade
3   Display Grade

Level 2
1.1 DO
1.2     RECEIVE Mark FROM KEYBOARD
1.3     IF Mark < 0 OR Mark > 100 THEN
1.4         SEND ["Error. Not possible!"] TO DISPLAY
1.5     END IF
1.6 UNTIL Mark >= 0 AND Mark <= 100

2.1 SELECT CASE Mark
2.2 CASE Mark >= 70
2.3     SET Grade TO "A"
2.4 CASE Mark 60 TO 69
2.5     SET Grade TO "B"
2.6 CASE Mark 50 TO 59
2.7     SET Grade TO "C"
2.8 CASE Mark 0 TO 49
2.9     SET Grade TO "FAIL"
2.10 END SELECT

3.1 FORMAT Grade
3.2 SEND ["The grade was: ", Grade] TO DISPLAY
```

DON'T FORGET

Never use programming keywords in pseudocode: e.g. 'Let Age = Inputbox("How old are you?")'.
Use ordinary English to convey the logic of the instruction: e.g. 'RECEIVE Mark FROM KEYBOARD', 'Enter Age from user' and so on.

ONLINE

There are many other methods of representing the design of a program, apart from structure diagrams and pseudocode. Try to find some others by entering 'software-design methodology' into a search engine.

 THINGS TO DO AND THINK ABOUT

The design stage of the software-development process addresses the user interface, structure and detailed logic of the software but is not concerned with the actual language in which the solution will be implemented.

Pseudocode should not use specific-language keywords but should show the same detailed logic using a more natural form of English.

ONLINE TEST

Test yourself on this topic online at www.brightredbooks.net

PHASES OF THE DEVELOPMENT PROCESS – INTRODUCTION AND ANALYSIS

INTRODUCTION

The development of a large-scale software project proceeds through several phases. The phases are: analysis, design, implementation, testing, documentation, evaluation and finally maintenance.

Analysis → Design → Implementation → Testing → Documentation → Evaluation → Maintenance

This spread, and the next three spreads (pages 22–29), will describe the details of what happens at each of these stages. The software-development process is often described as the software-development life cycle because, once a system has been developed, there will have to be a regeneration of the process to meet future needs, and in a sense the system is reborn.

DON'T FORGET

The development process is described as iterative, which means that earlier stages are often revisited for improvement in the light of experience gained at a later stage.

ONLINE

For further information on the software-development life cycle, follow the link at www.brightredbooks.net

PROJECT PROPOSAL

The project proposal (also known as a problem definition) is a document created following a preliminary meeting between the client and the systems analyst to discuss the existing system and to establish an early rapport with the client in order to understand their needs. The systems analyst will advise the client on the benefits of a new system and on the likely cost and time scale.

The project proposal is merely a rough outline of the problem and is in no way a legally binding document.

After the preliminary meeting and the production of the project proposal, the client will have a good idea of the cost and time scale for the project and of the potential benefits to the business. The client is now in a good position to decide whether to proceed with a full-scale analysis or to back out of the project without having incurred too much expenditure.

ANALYSIS

The software-development process begins with an analysis of the existing system. It is important that the needs of the client are clearly identified at this stage, otherwise time and money will be wasted at future stages in correcting mistakes in a system that does not do what it is supposed to do. In large organisations with complex systems, the analysis stage can take many months to complete.

At one time, the analysis was carried out by programmers who had very good technical skills but were not necessarily good at identifying and describing the client's needs. Nowadays, this stage is carried out by a systems analyst, who should have good technical skills as well as good communication skills.

TECHNIQUES USED AT THE ANALYSIS STAGE

The following are techniques used to extract information on the needs of the client.

Interviewing

The client will call meetings with key personnel within the business. Management and workers will be interviewed to obtain a whole picture of the needs of the clients. This is an opportunity to identify any problems with the existing system and to obtain a clear picture of what needs to be done.

Observation Notes

The day-to-day running of the business can be observed and notes made of what tasks people carry out in their role as part of the system.

Inspection of Existing Documentation

To gain an understanding of the needs of the system, existing documents can be inspected to examine how information is being collected and processed. Tracking how information changes over a period of time is often useful.

Questionnaires

Where it is not possible to interview staff directly, the indirect method of asking employees to complete a questionnaire can be used.

Software Specification

The software specification is a document produced at the end of the analysis stage. It is a result of an examination of the existing system and clearly identifying the needs of the client.

The software specification is:

1   a formal document which gives a clear and unambiguous description of exactly what the software has to do in order to meet the needs of the client.

2   a definition of the boundaries (time scale, budget etc.) of the problem. Defining the scope and boundaries of the problem allows the problem to be contained.

3   a document used as the basis for the design stage which follows next. In order to proceed with the design, every precise detail of the software has to be described in this document.

4   a legally binding contract between the developers and the client. If the final product does not meet the requirements as stated in the software specification, then this document can be used by the client in a court of law to support a legal action.

5   a description of the system at a logical level. It does not mention how the problem is to be solved or what hardware and software will be used in the solution to the problem.

ONLINE

Find out more information about software specification at www.brightredbooks.net

DON'T FORGET

The software specification is not the same as the project proposal. The software specification is an unambiguous detailed description of what the software must do, which forms a legally binding contract between the client and the developers. The project proposal is an initial outline of the problem to allow the client to decide if it is feasible to proceed with the project, and is not legally binding.

 THINGS TO DO AND THINK ABOUT

There is some confusion about the term **software specification**, which is also given the name **operational requirements document**. Both of these terms mean the same thing.

ONLINE TEST

Take the 'Phases of the Development Process' test at www.brightredbooks.net

PHASES OF THE DEVELOPMENT PROCESS – DESIGN AND IMPLEMENTATION

DESIGN

Once the analysis phase has been completed, the next phase in the software-development process is design. The software specification document that was agreed between the client and the developers as a result of the analysis phase is used as the basis for the design of the system.

There are three main stages to the design of the software:

1 design of the user interface
2 design of the structure of the software
3 design of the detailed logic of the software.

Wireframes, structure diagrams and pseudocode are used to represent these three elements of design. Details on these design notations are covered in the topic 'Design Notations' above.

IMPLEMENTATION

Once the design stage is complete, the next stage is to translate the design into a programming language. On a large-scale project, this will be done by a team of programmers led by a systems analyst.

The following points are guidelines for writing good code in the implementation of the solution, which will make it quicker to develop the software and easier to perform maintenance activities in the future.

1 The program should be modular (broken down into procedures and functions).
2 Variables should be given meaningful names such as 'Number1' and 'Country' as opposed to 'x' and 'y'.
3 Internal commentary should be used to explain the function of the code throughout the program listing.
4 Procedures and functions should not be too large and complicated.
5 Pre-written module libraries should be used to save time in the writing and testing of code.

CHOOSING A LANGUAGE

There is a wide choice of programming languages available.

Sometimes, a general-purpose package such as a spreadsheet or a database will be suitable for the solution, since these come with an interface already built in and offer a level of programming to extend the functionality of the basic package. On the other hand, implementing the solution in a programming language allows the solution to be completely customised to suit the user, without the limited programming constraints of a general-purpose package.

There are several factors that should be considered when choosing which programming language to use to implement the solution to the problem.

Some of the more important ones are given below:

1 The type of data (numeric, text, graphics, sound etc.) that the language has to support. For example, a scientific program that requires operations on large numbers would require a language that supports floating-point numbers.

2 The arithmetical and logical operations that are required, and whether the language supports these – for example, string operations to create substrings, join strings together and so on.

3 The operating-system environment in which the program will run. For example, some programming languages produce compiled programs that operate in a Windows environment.

4 The type of application that is being developed. For example, a multimedia authoring package would be chosen to develop a multimedia application, and a declarative language would be chosen to develop an expert system.

5 If the speed of execution of the software is important, then a language needs to be chosen that gives a solution with a fast response time.

6 The skills of the programming team must be considered, since there is little point in implementing the solution in a language of which the programmers have no experience.

 ONLINE

Most Scottish schools use Visual Basic to teach programming to students. There are several other languages that are popular at university level in computing courses. Use the internet to research the languages used at Scottish universities.

DON'T FORGET

Programming languages are very different in the types of data that they support and the operations on the data that they provide. Some languages are designed for specific purposes such as artificial intelligence or scientific areas, whereas others are general-purpose and can be used in a wide variety of applications.

DON'T FORGET

One or two of the terms used to describe a program are usually asked for in the knowledge-and-understanding component of the exam. To be sure of gaining full marks, learn the precise definitions given below, and don't steer too far away from them. For example, to explain the term 'correct' by saying that 'The program is free from errors' will gain no marks.

THINGS TO DO AND THINK ABOUT

The features of the language and the skills of the programmers are both important in choosing a programming language to implement a software solution to a problem.

Some programs are still written in a low-level language – which is very time-consuming and error-prone. Why is a low-level language sometimes the best choice of language?

 ONLINE TEST

Take the 'Phases of the Development Process' test at www.brightredbooks.net

PHASES OF THE DEVELOPMENT PROCESS – TESTING AND DOCUMENTATION

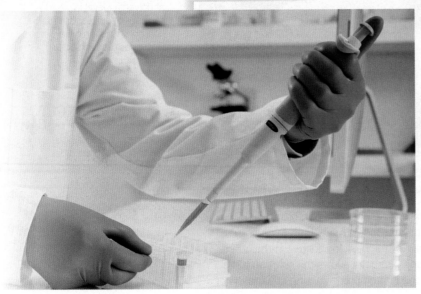

TESTING

The purpose of testing is to locate and remove errors.

One aspect of testing is to create a test plan and to choose test data that will comprehensively test the program for as many scenarios as time and cost will permit. This will involve selecting normal, extreme and exceptional test data. This aspect of testing has been dealt with in more detail in the spread entitled 'Testing'.

In a large software-development project, another aspect of testing is **systematic testing**. This involves a systematic progression through testing individual subprograms to testing the whole system.

SYSTEMATIC TESTING

Component Testing

The first stage is to check that individual procedures and functions work by themselves.

Module Testing

Once individual procedures and functions have been tested, the next stage is to test to see whether groups of procedures and functions successfully communicate with each other in modules.

Subsystem Testing

The systematic testing progresses on to test whether groups of modules work together as a unit in a subsystem.

System Testing

The whole system is tested to see whether the subsystems communicate together as a unit.

Acceptance Testing

Once the whole system has been tested by the developers, it is then tested by the clients in the situation in which it will be used.

DON'T FORGET

Module testing is also known as **integration testing**. Acceptance testing is also known as **beta testing**.

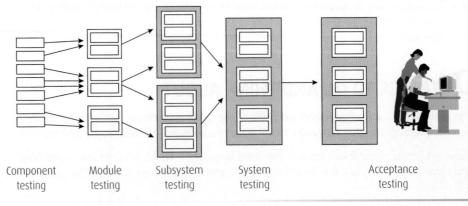

| Component testing | Module testing | Subsystem testing | System testing | Acceptance testing |

INDEPENDENT TEST GROUP

In general, programmers should not test their own programs, since they will be biased about exposing errors in their software, and often the testing will be incomplete and may allow errors to pass undetected.

A more rigorous approach to testing is to use **independent test groups** – outsiders who are trained in the task of finding errors.

DOCUMENTATION

Once the system has been implemented and fully tested, documentation is produced to help the users to learn how to use the system (the user guide), as well as documentation to help technical staff to install and maintain it (the technical guide).

The documentation traditionally was in the form of paper manuals but is now also commonly provided in electronic form, where it can be more easily updated to incorporate updates to the software. Other advantages of providing online help are that it can be searched quickly with keywords, and it is always available at the computer without the hassle of retrieving a manual.

Most software packages these days provide a small manual to get the user started, usually with a tutorial section and an extensive online help facility.

User Guide

This documentation in the user guide is provided to teach the user how to use the features of the software. It will contain a description of these features and will often include tutorials to lead the user through typical tasks such as inserting a new record or reordering items of stock.

Technical Guide

This documentation is provided to help technical staff to maintain the software. A large company will have an IT department who will take responsibility for the IT needs of the company. The following information would be included in this guide:

1   details on how to install the software
2   information on the amount of RAM, hard-disc capacity and processor requirements to run the software
3   the version number of the software
4   a reference section on troubleshooting, to help the user to identify and correct any system errors.

Other Documentation

The user guide and the technical guide are for the benefit of the client to make full use of their system. There are many documents produced during the stages of the software-development process. These documents are valuable as aids to the software-development team, who may well be involved in future maintenance of the system. Good documentation is essential for future maintenance of the system, since, before changes can be made, the existing system must be fully examined and understood.

These items of documentation will include items such as structured listings, pseudocode, structure charts, results of test runs, drawings of screen layouts and so on.

 THINGS TO DO AND THINK ABOUT

Documentation for a software solution exists in the form of a user guide, technical guide and documents produced during the development of the software.

Try to get hold of a software manual for a program that you use, and see what user and technical support it provides.

 **DON'T FORGET**

It is important to know the distinction between a user guide and a technical guide. The user guide describes how to use the features of the software, but the technical guide describes how to install and maintain it.

 ONLINE

Most companies provide online support on the internet for their products. Use a search engine to find out the online support that is available for Microsoft Word.

 DON'T FORGET

It is a common mistake to think that the user guide and the technical guide are the only items of documentation. Other items such as structured listings and pseudocode are equally important.

 **ONLINE TEST**

Take the 'Phases of the Development Process' test at www.brightredbooks.net

PHASES OF THE DEVELOPMENT PROCESS – EVALUATION AND MAINTENANCE

EVALUATION

When the software solution from analysis through to documentation is completed, it is important to evaluate it in terms of whether or not the original requirements have been met. Very often, the client is not happy with the final product, and so this stage is important to rectify as many weaknesses as possible in the software before it is delivered in its final form.

Terms Used to Describe a Program

- **Correct** – A program is correct if it meets the software specification. It can be described as fit for purpose, which means that it solves the problem it is supposed to solve.
- **Readable** – The program is easily understood by another programmer.
- **Reliable** – The program is free from design and coding errors.
- **Robust** – The program does not crash easily with unexpected input.
- **Maintainable** – A program is maintainable if future modifications can be performed easily and quickly.
- **Portable** – The program can be easily adapted to run in a different operating-system environment.
- **Efficient** – The size and speed of execution should be in proportion to the scale of the problem that it solves.

Judging criteria

The software is evaluated by judging it against a set of criteria. A list of criteria is drawn up that can be used to evaluate the system as it proceeds through the stages of analysis, design, implementation, testing and documentation.

Example:
At the design stage, criteria can be constructed to measure the quality of the user interface.
Does the client find the system user-friendly?
Can the software be learned to a competent level in 3 days?
Is there a consistency in the screen layouts?

Example:
At the implementation stage, criteria can be constructed to evaluate the quality of the structured listing.
Does the code use meaningful variable names?
Is the code efficient?
Does the code have sufficient internal commentary?

Example:
At the testing stage, criteria can be constructed to evaluate whether the testing has been carried out comprehensively.
Has testing been carried out with normal test data?
Has test data been used to test whether the software is robust?

ONLINE

Follow the link at www. brightredbooks.net to look up technical terms used throughout this book.

MAINTENANCE

Even after a software system is complete and up and running, it will still have to undergo changes in the future to reflect the changing needs of the clients or even to remove previously undetected errors that come to light once the system is put to work.

Maintenance falls into three categories:

Corrective Maintenance

This involves removing errors in the software that were not detected during development but have come to light later when the clients are using the system. These errors should be removed by the development team.

contd

Adaptive Maintenance

Over time, the software and hardware environment in which the system runs can change. For example, the operating system could be updated to a newer version, or different hardware devices such as barcode scanners or graph plotters could be employed.

The software system will require adaptive maintenance to adapt to these changes.

Perfective Maintenance

At some point in the future, the client may request added enhancements to the software. This may be to modify the system by improving existing functions of the software or to add extra features to respond to changing needs of the system.

COSTS

The client will not incur costs for corrective maintenance, since the developers have not met the legally binding contract stated in the software specification. However, any adaptive or perfective maintenance involves changes to the system outside the original agreement, and the client must pay for these maintenance activities.

FACTORS AFFECTING MAINTENANCE

Staff Mobility

People change jobs for a variety of reasons. Often, the staff who developed the original system have moved to another job, and new staff are required to perform maintenance on the software. This makes maintenance more difficult, since the new staff will require time to familiarise themselves with a system that they did not create.

Poor Documentation

To modify a piece of software requires an understanding of how it works. Incomplete or outdated documentation acts as a hindrance to maintenance. Any modifications to a system should also be incorporated into the documentation for the system.

Module Independence

Module independence is achieved by minimising the number of input and output parameters that the modules require, and by using local variables instead of global variables wherever possible.

Modules should be made as independent of each other as possible, so that changes to one module do not require changes to all other modules that share the same data.

Programming Language

Some programming languages, by their nature, are easier to maintain than others. For example, a low-level-language program is much harder to modify than a high-level-language program.

Programming Style

Programs that are readable by using internal commentary, meaningful variable names, indented loops etc. are easier to understand and hence to maintain than others.

Hardware and Software Stability

If the hardware used by the software is being changed, or the operating system that the software runs on is being frequently upgraded to a new version, then the software may require modifications.

 THINGS TO DO AND THINK ABOUT

During the lifetime of a system, approximately 20% of time is spent on corrective, 20% of time on adaptive and 60% of time on perfective maintenance.

DEVELOPMENT METHODOLOGIES

INTRODUCTION

When writing the short programs required for this course, it is possible to proceed with producing the software without spending too much time on planning. However, in a large-scale commercial project involving teams of programmers, meetings with clients and generating vast amounts of documentation, it is essential that the process be planned.

A software-development methodology is a framework that is used to structure, plan and control the process of developing a software project. Most development methodologies have an overall theme which involves a suite of techniques rather than one principle.

There are dozens of development methodologies, but in this course you are only expected to know these three:

1 Top-down design/Stepwise refinement

2 Agile development methodology

3 Rapid application development.

ONLINE

Use a search engine to look into other software-development methodologies such as Waterfall, Crystal, Scrum and Spiral.

TOP-DOWN DESIGN/STEPWISE REFINEMENT

Top-down design methodology starts with the main program and breaks it down progressively into logical, manageable modules. The process proceeds in steps through levels of refinement until the parts can be dealt with individually.

The principles of this methodology are addressed in more detail in the spread entitled 'Design Notations' above.

The client is involved in meetings at the analysis phase, but no further interaction takes place with the client until the beta testing of the completed software.

AGILE DEVELOPMENT METHODOLOGY

Agile software development is a methodology that anticipates the need for flexibility and regular adaptions to changing circumstances. It is a response to the problems that can arise when a large-scale application is delivered at the end of the development process without consulting the client as the project proceeds. This methodology focuses on delivering parts of the solution as soon as they are ready. By delivering parts of the application as the project progresses, the client is involved all the way through development and can give the developers meaningful feedback on any problems. The parts of the program then come together to make the complete software solution.

Agile development methodologies are commonly used in the development of computer games.

AGILE CONCEPTS

Client Collaboration

It is very difficult to collect the complete requirements of a large-scale project at the beginning of the software-development process. So, it is important to keep the client involved in the process. There should be daily meetings between the clients and the developers, and necessary changes made to the requirements even late in development.

Most agile teams are located in a shared office space and include all the people necessary to develop the software. The team will include programmers and the people who manage the project, such as project managers, systems analysts and the clients.

Individuals and Interactions

Self-organisation and motivation are important, as well as interactions such as developers working in a shared location and programmers working in pairs. The principle is that face-to-face conversation is a better form of communication than e-mailing and telephone calls.

RAPID APPLICATION DEVELOPMENT (RAD)

The Rapid Application Development methodology was developed in response to the need to deliver systems very fast. One problem with previous methodologies was that applications took so long to build that the requirements had changed before the system was complete, which resulted in poor-quality or sometimes unusable systems. However, the RAD approach is not appropriate to all projects. For example, an air-traffic-control system or missile-control system produced by RAD would not instil much confidence!

The objective of RAD is to build a small-scale prototype of the finished product in a short period of time for the purpose of eliciting the user's requirements and to make any necessary changes to the requirements. The initial prototype then goes through a series of incremental updates where extra features and functions are added as a result of feedback from the client until the final product is achieved.

RAD reduces development time by using the following techniques:

- A lack of extensive pre-planning, which allows software to be written much faster and makes it easier to change requirements.
- Producing prototypes for the user to test designs, so that errors and problems are identified early on in the process. Prototyping also helps in developing a system that closely addresses the needs of the client.
- Reusing software components rather than creating them from scratch.
- Keeping review meetings and other team communication informal to reduce the amount of time and documentation generated by the project.

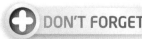 **DON'T FORGET**

Rapid Application Development (RAD) is a software-development methodology that focuses on building applications in a very short amount of time. Inherent in this approach, there may be a compromise in factors such as functionality, quality of the interface and execution speed.

 THINGS TO DO AND THINK ABOUT

There are similarities and differences in software-development methodologies. For example, rapid application and agile methodologies both promote communication with the client as the project proceeds. However, the main emphasis in RAD is on speed of production, whereas Agile is concerned with flexibility and response to change.

 ONLINE TEST

Test yourself on this topic online at www.brightredbooks.net

VIRTUAL MACHINES, EMULATORS AND MOBILE DEVICES

INTRODUCTION

A computer that exists in the real world has an operating system that manages the hardware and software of the computer system. Activities such as writing to a hard disc, sending data to a printer, allocating an area of memory to a program while it is running, or sending data for transmission to a Network Interface Card (NIC) are all tasks performed by the operating system.

Sometimes, it can be useful to make one type of computer function as if it was another type of computer – to run a program which was written for another machine, or to run programs for which the real hardware is not available to run it.

VIRTUAL MACHINE

A virtual machine is a computer that runs software to emulate the functions of a real-world computer.

A virtual machine can be used by organisations to run software applications that are not available for the operating-system platform used by the real computers. For example, an organisation could have a network of computers running Windows but need to run a graphics-editing program which only runs on the Mac OS operating system. In this situation, a computer can act as a host for the guest computer and run the application without the need to purchase an Apple computer.

A guest operating system is installed, executed and powered entirely by the machine hosting it. The guest virtual machine runs simultaneously with the machine that is hosting it. One host operating system can run several guest operating systems at the same time.

The guest and the host share hardware resources, but the guest virtual machine has a separate guest operating system which executes on top of the host machine operating system through a program called a **hypervisor**.

The hypervisor manages the running of one or more guest operating systems on a single host computer at the same time.

The initial cost of virtualisation can be high, but the ongoing costs are lower than using several physical computers, since money is saved in maintenance, energy consumption and the cost of space to house the hardware.

The virtualisation of server computers on a network is commonplace, since several server functions can be hosted on a host server computer. For example, a server can be used to host file server, print server, multimedia server etc. guests instead of providing the different functions on several server computers.

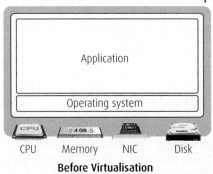

Before Virtualisation

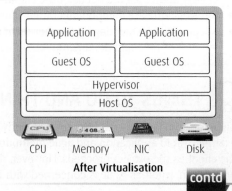

After Virtualisation

contd

VIDEO LINK

Head to www. brightredbooks.net to watch a video explaining the basic concept of a hypervisor.

DON'T FORGET

A physical computer on which a hypervisor is running one or more virtual machines is defined as a **host machine**. Each virtual machine is called a **guest machine**.

Advantages

- One physical computer is used to act and perform like other computers, so money is saved on hardware.
- Energy consumption is reduced, since there are fewer computers being powered.
- Less space is required to house several computers.
- There is more flexibility and ability to respond quickly to change.
- Disaster recovery, for example in the event of a fire, is improved, since one host computer can be replaced and the necessary software reinstalled, as opposed to replacing and configuring several computers.

Disadvantages

- A virtual machine is not as efficient as a real one, since hardware components are accessed indirectly.
- Running several virtual machines at the same time on a host computer can result in poor performance and instability.

EMULATORS

An emulator is a software application that accurately imitates an item of computing hardware such as a hard disc drive, a mobile phone or an arcade video-games machine.

Disc Image

An example of an emulator is a disc image which is a duplicate of a storage device such as an optical disc, hard drive, tape drive and so on. The emulated drive is typically created on a hard drive, or sometimes in RAM if fast read/write access is required.

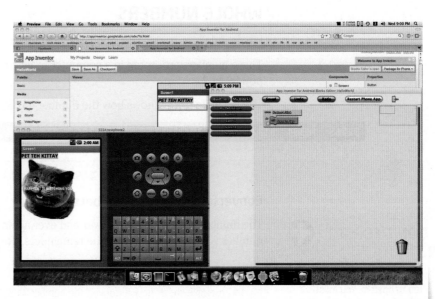

Disc images are used for backup and upgrades to computer systems. In case of computer failure, a backup disc image can be used to recover the computer system or to find and restore any important files from a disc image.

Classic video games from the 1970s can be reproduced faithfully on a modern computer by creating an image of the original game's ROM and disc data.

MOBILE DEVICES

A mobile device such as a tablet computer or a smartphone is essentially a small-scale emulation of a computer system. Essentially, it has the same architecture, has similar machine code and is programmed in a similar way. There are similarities and differences (screen size, memory, clock speed, operating systems etc.) in how different types of computer operate, from simple microprocessor devices through smartphones and tablets to larger computers.

 **ONLINE**

App Inventor is a program that emulates a mobile phone on a computer to build an app. Head to www. brightredbooks.net to watch tutorials and download software to do this.

 THINGS TO DO AND THINK ABOUT

 ONLINE TEST

How well have you learned this topic? Take the test at www.brightredbooks.net

Your school will almost certainly be using a virtual server rather than several real servers to manage the school computer network. Ask your teacher or the network manager for an explanation of how the network is configured in this respect.

REPRESENTATION OF NUMBERS

ONLINE

Use a search engine to investigate other units that are used in computing, such as 'nibble', exabyte and zettabyte.

INTRODUCTION

A computer uses electricity to represent two states, which are current ON and current OFF.

Binary numbers have two digits, 1 (current ON) and 0 (current off), which can be used to represent the instructions and data in a computer.

UNITS

A bit is a binary digit	(1 or 0)
A byte is a group of 8 bits	(e.g. 10101001)
A kilobyte (Kb) is 1,024 bytes	(2^{10} bytes)
A megabyte (Mb) is 1,024 kilobytes = 1,048,576 bytes	(2^{20} bytes)
A gigabyte (Gb) is 1,024 megabytes = 1,073,741,824 bytes	(2^{30} bytes)
A terabyte (Tb) is 1,024 gigabytes = 1,099,511,627,776 bytes	(2^{40} bytes)
A petabyte (Pb) is 1,024 terabytes = 1,125,899,906,842,624 bytes	(2^{50} bytes)

WHOLE NUMBERS

Whole numbers include zero and positive numbers but not fractions, i.e. 0, 1, 2, 3, 4, 5, 6, 7 ...

These numbers are stored in a computer in **binary**, which is a number system based on powers of 2.

The example below shows how the number 45,685 is stored in 16-bit binary.

32768	16384	8192	4096	2048	1024	512	256	128	64	32	16	8	4	2	1
1	0	1	1	0	0	1	0	0	1	1	1	0	1	0	1

32,768 + 8,192 + 4,096 + 512 + 64 + 32 + 16 + 4 + 1 = 45,685

Conversion of Whole Numbers to Binary

The number is divided by two over and over again until zero is reached. The binary number is then obtained from the remainders. (Read the remainders from bottom to top.)

DON'T FORGET

It is a common mistake to read the remainders from top to bottom. You must read the remainders **from bottom to top**.

VIDEO LINK

Watch the tutorial on the binary counting system at www.brightredbooks.net

Example:

This example shows how to convert the number 41,800 into 16-bit binary:

2	41800	
2	20900	R 0
2	10450	R 0
2	5225	R 0
2	2612	R 1
2	1306	R 0
2	653	R 0
2	326	R 1
2	163	R 0
2	81	R 1
2	40	R 1
2	20	R 0
2	10	R 0
2	5	R 0
2	2	R 1
2	1	R 0
2	0	R 1

Answer: 1010001101001000

RANGE OF NUMBERS

The number of different binary numbers that can be represented in a given number of bits is shown in the table.

No. of bits	Numbers	No. of numbers
1	0, 1	2
2	00, 01, 10, 11	4
3	000, 001, 010, 011, 100, 101, 110, 111	8
...	...	...
8	...	256
N		2^N

Number of bits	8	16	24	32
Range of numbers	$0...2^8 - 1$	$0...2^{16} - 1$	$0...2^{24} - 1$	$0...2^{32} - 1$

DON'T FORGET

It is a common mistake to think that 2^N is the largest whole number in N bits. The largest number is 1 less than 2^N, since the numbers start at zero and not at 1. For example, 16 bits can store 2^{16} numbers. This gives a range of numbers from 0 to $2^{16} - 1$ (0...65,535).

INTEGERS

Integers include positive and negative numbers, but not fractions: i.e. ...–2, –1, 0, 1, 2 ... Computers use a system called **two's complement** to store integers. The most significant bit represents (–128), and the remaining bits are the same as for whole numbers.

Example:

This example shows how the number (–83) is stored in 8-bit two's complement.

-128	64	32	16	8	4	2	1
1	0	1	0	1	1	0	1

–128 + 32 + 8 + 4 + 1 = (–83)

The table below shows the range of numbers that can be represented in 8-bit two's complement.

	-128	64	32	16	8	4	2	1	
Largest	0	1	1	1	1	1	1	1	127
Smallest	1	0	0	0	0	0	0	0	-128

VIDEO LINK

Have a look at floating-point numbers at www.brightredbooks.net

ONLINE

Use a search engine to investigate the difference in the representation of **single** and **double** data types in the Visual Basic programming language.

REAL NUMBERS

Real numbers include **decimal fractions** as well as **integers**, e.g. 7, –2, 518·2, –8·127, 0·047. Computers use a system called **floating point** to store real numbers. The floating-point number is made up of the **mantissa**, which holds the significant figures of the number, and the **exponent**, which holds the power.

Example:

$$\boxed{\text{Mantissa}} \rightarrow 0·10110011 \times 2^{11101001} \leftarrow \boxed{\text{Exponent}}$$

An advantage of floating-point notation is that very large and very small numbers can be stored in a small number of bits.

A disadvantage of floating-point notation is that accuracy is lost, since the mantissa only gives the number to a certain amount of significant figures.

Accuracy and Range of Floating-Point Numbers

Increasing the number of bits assigned to the mantissa increases the accuracy.
Increasing the number of bits assigned to the exponent increases the range of numbers.

 THINGS TO DO AND THINK ABOUT

Computers use different representations for different types of numbers. Integers are stored in two's complement notation, and real numbers are stored as floating-point numbers.

ONLINE TEST

Test yourself on this topic online at www.brightredbooks.net

REPRESENTATION OF GRAPHICS

August 2014 £3.70

The world's leading sugarcraft magazine

Cake
CRAFT & DECORATION

Summer Fun

Step-by-Step projects

Sports models
- cricket, football, rubgy and tennis

Carved giraffes

Baby shower cake

- Enter NEC 2014 competitions
- Geranium

STEP-BY-STEP PROJECTS FOR ALL SKILL LEVELS

www.cake-craft.com

INTRODUCTION

Images appear widely in glossy magazines, catalogues, websites, newspapers and so on. These images have probably been captured by a digital camera or scanner and then input into a computer system. Graphics-editing programs can then be used to manipulate the graphics into a desired image.

There are two types of graphics program – called **bit-mapped** graphics and **vector** graphics. Each of these programs stores and edits an image in different ways.

BIT-MAPPED GRAPHICS

This type of graphics stores an image as colour codes for a two-dimensional grid of pixels. The term **pixel** comes from 'picture element' and is the dots that make up the graphic.

Bit-mapped graphics programs will have tools such as a rubber and a paint spraycan so that the colour of individual pixels can be changed.

Bit Depth

The bit depth is the number of bits that are used as the code for the colour of each pixel.

The simplest bit depth is 1 bit, which can encode two colours (usually black and white), since 1 bit has two codes (1 and 0), which can be used to represent both colours.

An image using 8-bit depth will be able to represent $2^8 = 256$ colours.

An image using 24-bit depth will be able to represent $2^{24} = 16,777,216$ colours.

A bit depth of 24 bits is called **true** colour, since it represents the limit of the number of colours that the human eye can recognise. This is a commonly used bit depth for bit mapped graphics programs.

Resolution

The resolution is the size of the pixels and is usually measured in dots per inch (dpi).

High-resolution graphics are made up of a large number of small pixels.

Low-resolution graphics are made up of a small number of large pixels.

Resolution is a factor that will affect the quality of an image. High-resolution graphics will have more detail than low-resolution graphics and will consequently produce a more accurate image. The drawback is that high-resolution graphics have larger storage requirements.

DON'T FORGET ➕

The number of colour codes that result from a bit depth of N bits is derived from the formula 2^N.
Remember that a bit depth of 16 bits does not result in 16 colours but in 2^{16} (65,536) colours.

Low resolution

High resolution

contd

Calculation of Storage Requirements of Bit-mapped Graphics

Example:

This example shows the calculation for the storage requirements of a bit-mapped graphic.

You should always give your answer in a suitable unit. In this example, it is better to give an answer of 27·5 megabytes rather than millions of bytes.

600 dpi
256 colours

8 inches

10 inches

Storage requirements
= 8 × 10 × 600 × 600 × 8 bits (2^8=256)
= 230,400,000 bits
= 28,800,000 bytes
= 27·5 Mb

ONLINE

Find out more about graphics at www. brightredbooks.net

VECTOR GRAPHICS

This type of graphics stores an image as a list of objects, each of which is described by its attributes.

The attributes are features that describe an object, such as its starting coordinates, length, fill colour, line thickness and so on.

For example, the image shown alongside consists of Rectangle, Circle and Textbox objects.

Each object is stored by its attributes:

e.g.   Rectangle: start x, start y, length, breadth, fill colour, line colour, line thickness, line pattern etc.

       Circle: centre x, centre y, radius, fill colour, line colour, line thickness etc.

       Textbox: start x, start y, text, font, fontsize, fill colour, line colour, line thickness etc.

Bit-mapped Graphics vs Vector Graphics

- Bit-mapped graphics in general have a larger storage requirement than vector graphics, since the colour codes for thousands or millions of pixels have to be stored.
- Vector graphics only need to store codes for the objects and attributes that the image is composed of.
- A bit-mapped image will become pixellated and jagged when enlarged, since the resolution is fixed for the original image.
- A vector graphic will not become pixellated, since the resolution is not fixed and the objects' attributes are simply changed to match the enlarged objects.
- Parts of a bit-mapped graphic cannot be separated without leaving blank areas of pixels, but in vector graphics overlapping objects can be separated or layered in different orders.
- Bit-mapped graphics can be edited in fine detail by editing individual pixels, but vector graphics are edited by changing the attributes of objects.

ONLINE

Adobe Photoshop is a commercially available package used widely to edit bit-mapped graphics. Investigate the maximum pixel dimension of images supported by this software at www.brightredbooks.net

 THINGS TO DO AND THINK ABOUT

Bit-mapped and vector graphics each store images in very different ways. A complex image made up of varying pixels needs to be created with bit-mapped graphics, but an image that is made up of basic shapes, such as a chessboard, should be created with vector graphics.

ONLINE TEST

Take the 'Representation of Graphics' test at www. brightredbooks.net

REPRESENTATION OF CHARACTERS, VIDEO, SOUND AND INSTRUCTIONS

CHARACTERS

Text in a computer system is represented by using a binary code for each character.

ASCII and Unicode are two standards that have been developed for text representation. These standards have been developed so that textual data can be transferred between different computer programs. If different programs used different binary codes for each character, then text could not be transferred between programs without the need for some form of translation, which would take time.

ASCII (AMERICAN CODE FOR STANDARD INFORMATION INTERCHANGE)

The ASCII system is based on the English alphabet and represents each character in 8 bits. The most significant bit (first bit from the left) is called a **parity bit** and is used for error-checking. The remaining 7 bits are used to encode the character.

The example shows how the character 'A' is represented in ASCII.

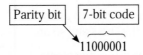

The ASCII system allows for $2^7 = 128$ different codes. This is sufficient to represent the 26 uppercase and 26 lowercase letters, a few dozen punctuation characters, the symbols for the digits 0, 1, 2, 3...9, and control characters that are all found in the English language.

Control characters are special non-printing characters used for special purposes such as Return, Tab and End of file. These characters each have their own ASCII code.

Parity Bit

Parity is an error-detection technique used to detect errors in the transmission of a single character.

If odd parity is used, then the parity bit will be set so that the number of 1s in the byte is always an odd number.

An even parity check means that the parity bit will be set so that the number of 1s in the byte is always an even number. The examples below are illustrated using odd parity.

DON'T FORGET

The ASCII system represents 128 characters and not 256 characters, since 1 bit is used as a parity check, so that only 7 bits of the bits are used for the character code.

If a character is sent and a bit gets corrupted from a 1 to a 0, then the receiver will not receive a byte with odd parity and can detect that an error has occurred and will then send a request that the character be retransmitted.

UNICODE

The ASCII code language is limited in that it can only store 128 characters. This is fine for the English alphabet but does not cater for characters in foreign languages throughout the world such as Japanese, Arabic and so on.

contd

The Unicode system is a solution to this problem in that it uses 16 bits to encode each character, allowing for $2^{16} = 65,536$ codes.

Comparison of ASCII and Unicode:

- ASCII has fewer storage requirements than Unicode, since ASCII uses 1 byte to store each character, whereas Unicode uses 2 bytes.
- Unicode can store $2^{16} = 65,536$ characters; ASCII can only store $2^7 = 128$ characters.

ONLINE

For a deeper explanation of ASCII and Unicode, follow the link at www.brightredbooks.net and enter 'ASCII' and 'Unicode' as keywords.

VIDEO

Video on a computer system is achieved by showing a sequence of still frames many times per second.

Typically, a frame rate of 25 frames per second is sufficient to create smooth motion.

The quality of the video will depend on the frame rate and on the resolution and bit depth of each frame.

The bit depth is the number of bits allocated to encode the colour of each pixel.

The resolution is measured either in dots per inch (dpi) or by describing the dimension of a frame in pixels, e.g. 768 x 576.

SOUND

Digital sound is described in terms of the sample size and the sample rate. The sample rate is a measure of how often a sample is taken. Sample size indicates how much information is taken in each sample.

Binary codes are used to describe the pitch and volume of the sound. The sample size is how many bits are used to describe the sound in one sample. The two most common sample sizes are 16-bit and 24-bit samples. A higher sample size represents the sound with greater definition.

Sample rates are measured in KHz, which is many thousands of times per second. The higher the sample rate, the smoother the transition between samples, and hence a better quality of sound.

How closely the digitised sound matches the original depends upon the sampling rate and the sample size.

DON'T FORGET

The bit depth and the resolution of a single video frame is equivalent to the bit depth and resolution of a still bit-map image. Think of video as being a series of bit-map images.

INSTRUCTIONS (MACHINE CODE)

Machine code is a set of instructions encoded in binary patterns which are executed directly by a computer's central processing unit (CPU). Each instruction performs a specific task, such as loading an item of data from a memory location into the processor, performing an ALU operation on an item of data or branching to a specific instruction.

Every processor or family of processors has its own machine-code set of instructions.

ONLINE

Explore how data is stored in the computer further at www.brightredbooks.net

ONLINE TEST

How well have you learned this topic? Take the test at www.brightredbooks.net

 THINGS TO DO AND THINK ABOUT

Binary codes are used in a computer to represent both data and programs. Numbers, text, graphics, video and sound data are represented by binary codes, as are the machine-code instruction of the programs.

COMPUTER ARCHITECTURE 1

VIDEO LINK

Watch the video showing an overview of computer architecture at www. brightredbooks.net

ONLINE

Follow the link at www. brightredbooks.net for a more detailed description of CPU architecture.

PROCESSOR(S)

A computer solves a problem by storing a set of instructions (a program) in memory that are then fetched and executed one at a time to solve a problem. This is called the **'stored program concept'**.

The diagram below shows the basic components of a computer system.

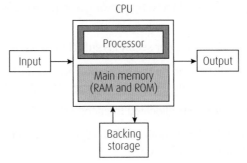

The CPU (central processing unit) is made up of a processor chip and main-memory chips.

The processor is responsible for fetching and executing instructions held in main memory, one at a time.

The processor is made up of **three** components:

1   Control unit
2   Arithmetic and logic unit (ALU)
3   Registers.

Control Unit

The control unit is responsible for initiating the fetching, decoding and execution of instructions by sending out signals to other parts of the computer system.

ALU (Arithmetic Logic Unit)

The ALU carries out arithmetic operations (+, −, *, /) and logical operations such as AND, OR, NOT and so on.

Processor Registers

Registers are individual storage locations on the processor which hold an instruction, data or the address of a memory location.

The Instruction Register (IR) holds the instruction that is currently being executed by the processor.

The Accumulator (A) is a data register which holds the accumulated results of calculations performed in the ALU.

The Program Counter (PC) is a register which holds the address of the main-memory location storing the next instruction to be executed by the program.

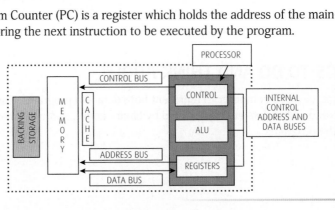

MULTI-CORE PROCESSORS

Processors were originally developed with only one core, which meant that they could only execute one instruction at any given instant. In recent years, there has been a move towards multi-core processors, i.e. a single chip with two or more processor components (called **cores**) which can independently execute program instructions.

Multi-core processors can execute multiple instructions at the same time, thus increasing the overall speed of program execution.

Manufacturers typically integrate several cores onto a single integrated circuit. A dual-core processor has two cores (e.g. AMD Phenom II X2; Intel Core Duo), while a quad-core processor contains four cores (e.g. AMD Phenom II X4; Intel's quad-core processors). Eight-core processors and beyond exist which are suited to running applications where a high-performance computer system is required, such as high-resolution gaming.

DON'T FORGET

A processor register only holds a single item of data. Do not confuse this with main memory, which holds data items in millions of memory locations.

ONLINE

Follow the link at www. brightredbooks.net to investigate the technology of processor chips.

MEMORY

Main memory stores the programs and data that are currently being executed.

It consists of RAM and ROM chips.

RAM (Random-access Memory)

RAM is volatile (loses its contents when the power is switched off).

RAM can be read from and written to. When a program is loaded from the hard disc to be run, the program instructions are written into RAM.

There are two types of RAM: **static** RAM and **dynamic** RAM.

Static RAM keeps its contents so long as power is maintained to the chip, but dynamic RAM requires to be refreshed every few milliseconds by rewriting its contents – as well as power being supplied. Dynamic RAM has simpler circuitry than static RAM and needs less power. Consequently, dynamic RAM is cheaper than static RAM. The main advantage of static RAM over dynamic RAM is that it has faster access.

ROM (Read-only Memory)

ROM is non-volatile (keeps its contents when the power is switched off).

The programs in ROM are put into the chip when it is manufactured, and are permanent. The instructions in ROM can be read by the processor, but they are never written to.

A small part of the operating system which is executed at start-up, called the **BIOS** (Basic Input/Output System), is stored in ROM.

DON'T FORGET

There are a lot of acronyms used in this course. Make sure that you know them all – but also remember that expanding an acronym is not sufficient to answer a question such as: 'What is the function of RAM?'

THINGS TO DO AND THINK ABOUT

Computing hardware is constantly developing in performance, and new technologies are constantly appearing. You are not expected to have a detailed knowledge of the thousands of IT devices that are currently available. However, you should read computing magazines and visit websites (PC World, Dell etc.) to get a feel for the current specification of devices. This will widen your understanding and will allow you to bring more depth to your answers.

ONLINE TEST

Head to www. brightredbooks.net and take the 'Computer Architecture' test.

COMPUTER ARCHITECTURE 2

VIDEO LINK

Learn more about a computer cache at www. brightredbooks.net

CACHE

This is an area of fast-access memory either between the processor and main memory or on the processor chip itself. The cache holds instructions and data that are used most frequently. Since these are in fast-access storage, it increases the overall performance of the system.

PROCESSOR BUSES

The CPU has buses, which are multiple wires/lines that connect the processor and main memory. They are used to carry data, to specify memory-location addresses, and to send signals between them.

Data Bus

This bus is used to transfer data between main memory and the processor. It is a **two-way** bus, since data can be transferred from a memory location to the processor and vice versa.

Early computers had a data bus that was 8 lines wide and transferred 8 bits in a single operation. Modern desktop computers will typically have a 64-bit data bus.

The number of bits that the processor transfers in one operation is called the **word size**.

Address Bus

This bus is used to specify the address of the memory location that is to be read from or written to. This bus is a **one-way** bus, since the processor will use it to specify which memory location it is going to use; but the reverse does not apply.

Early computers had an address bus that was 16 lines wide. Modern desktop computers will typically have a 32-bit address bus.

Control Bus

Each of the control-bus lines has a specific function. Here are the functions of some control-bus lines:

- *Read* – A signal down this line is used to initiate a **memory READ** operation, which reads the contents of a memory location into the processor.
- *Write* – A signal down this line is used to initiate a **memory WRITE** operation, which writes an item of data from the processor into a memory location.
- *Clock* – The clock line sends a regular series of pulses into the processor to synchronise events. The time interval between each pulse is called a **clock cycle**. For example, a memory read or a memory write takes place in one clock cycle.
- *Reset* – A signal down this line causes the computer to stop execution of the current program and then to reboot.
- *Interrupt* – Peripheral devices, such as printers, can send a signal on the interrupt line into the processor when they require attention. This causes the processor to deal with the interrupting device.

DON'T FORGET

The control bus is not really a bus at all, in the sense that it is made up of a number of individual lines, each of which has its own specific function. This is different from the data and address buses, where all the lines work together as a unit to code an item of data or an address.

DON'T FORGET

The three processor buses all play a role in a memory READ or WRITE operation. It is important to know the order in which the steps take place, and not just a general description of the process.

MEMORY READ AND WRITE OPERATIONS

Memory READ

A processor reads instructions from memory as part of the **fetch–execute cycle**, or reads items of data to perform a calculation.

Step 1   The processor sets up the address bus with the address of the required memory location.

contd

Step 2   The processor activates the READ line on the control bus.
Step 3   The contents of the memory location are transferred along the data bus into the processor.
Step 4   If it is an instruction, it is decoded and executed.

Memory WRITE

Step 1   The processor sets up the address bus with the address of the required memory location.
Step 2   The processor sets up the data bus with the data to be written to memory.
Step 3   The processor activates the WRITE line on the control bus.
Step 4   The data is transferred along the data bus to the memory location.

CALCULATION OF MAIN MEMORY CAPACITY

A processor with a 32-bit address bus and a 24-bit data bus can create 2^{32} = 4,294,967,296 addresses. There are 2^{32} addressable memory locations; and each holds 24 bits.

The maximum memory size that this processor can support is 2^{32} x 24 bits = 2^{32} x 3 bytes = 12 Gb.

INTERFACE

An interface is a combination of the hardware and software between the processor and a device to allow for their differences in speed and operation.

Physical Connection

Typically, this will be a wired connection; but wireless connections are becoming more frequent.

Data Format Conversion

The CPU stores data in a different format from the peripheral device. For example, the voltage levels representing 1 and 0 can vary, and analogue-to-digital conversion may be required.

Data-format conversion can also involve the conversion of **serial** data to **parallel** data.

In a **serial** interface, each bit of data is transferred one bit after another down a single line.

In a **parallel** interface, multiple bits are transferred down parallel lines at the same time.

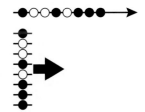

Data Storage

The interface provides an area to store data until the slower peripheral device is ready to accept it.

Status Information

The interface provides information on the current state of the device. For example, a printer interface will provide information such as: ready to accept more data, printer out of paper, toner low and so on.

Protocol Conversion

A protocol is a set of rules agreed between a sender and receiver so that they can successfully communicate with each other. The interface may require to convert protocols so that the CPU and the device can communicate.

 ONLINE

Use a search engine to investigate the difference in speed between the USB 2 and USB 3 interfaces.

 THINGS TO DO AND THINK ABOUT

 ONLINE TEST

Head to www. brightredbooks.net and take the 'Computer Architecture' test.

Increasing the clock speed, the width of the data bus, the width of the address bus, processor cache and improved interfaces have all improved the performance of computer systems dramatically over the last few decades.

The trend has been for increased processor speed, larger-capacity main memory and backing storage, and faster data transfers between the CPU and peripheral devices.

CONTEMPORARY DEVELOPMENTS

INTRODUCTION

Computing is an area where the technology is constantly changing and developing. Computer systems of today are at the same time different from, and yet similar to, systems of a few decades ago. There are trends that can be identified in the direction of change of computing technologies.

SOFTWARE-DEVELOPMENT LANGUAGES AND ENVIRONMENTS

Trend Towards Higher-level Languages

The historical development of programming languages has proceeded in the order shown in the table.

Generation	Language type
First generation	Machine code
Second generation	Assembly language
Third generation	High-level language
Fourth generation	Fourth-generation language (4GL)

Machine code and assembly language are both called **low-level languages**.

Before the existence of high-level programming languages, computers were programmed in machine code using binary codes. This was a monotonous task which was very error-prone.

This led to the development of assembly languages that made programming easier but still required specialist technical ability.

High-level programming languages appeared in the 1950s, supporting features such as data types, control structures, functions/procedures, parameters and so on.

The trend towards a higher level of language then proceeded to fourth-generation languages, which use language that is closer to human languages than typical high-level programming languages are.

They were designed in such a way that users could specify the nature of the problem without having to understand the technical details of the underlying code.

A typical command in 4GL would take the form:

    SELECT ALL RECORDS WHERE NAME IS "WENDY"

Trend Towards Specialised Languages

Initially, software applications were created with general-purpose languages, where the programmer used the available features of the language to develop software in a particular area. There are now a vast number of specialised languages with features and functions that are tailor-made to a specific area. For example, a control language that programs a robot arm has commands that relate to the parts of the robot (WAIST ROTATE 180, GRIPPER CLOSE etc.).

Control Constructs

Early programming languages had control constructs for sequencing (INPUT...INPUT...LET), selection (IF...THEN...ELSE...END IF) and repetition (REPEAT...UNTIL), since these constructs are essential to solve problems efficiently. They also had user-defined procedures and functions.

There has been a trend towards increasing the number of programming constructs available in languages in order to maximise the efficiency and readability of the code.

These include other branching constructs such as SELECT CASE...END CASE, and extra loops such as WHILE...END WHILE.

contd

Software-development Environment

'Software-development environment' refers to the hardware and software tools that are used to build software systems. Over the last couple of decades, the set of software tools available to developers has expanded considerably.

There has been a move towards graphical programming environments, where programs are created by manipulating program elements graphically rather than by specifying them textually. Visual Basic is a language in which the programmer drags and drops command buttons, text boxes, picture boxes etc. onto the program interface and then writes code for these elements.

Current software-development environments usually include a set of debugging tools such as trace tables and breakpoints, and include text-editors that automatically format code.

INTELLIGENT SYSTEMS

Increasing Use of Robotics and Autonomous Unmanned Vehicles

Since 2009 or so, robot sales have steadily increased by 9% on average per year to match the trend towards automation all over the world.

Common industrial applications are in car-manufacturing robots, underwater robots, demolition robots and surgical robots. There is also a massive untapped potential for domestic chores such as mowing the lawn and vacuuming the carpets.

Increasing processing power and improving artificial-intelligence (AI) techniques such as image recognition, touch-sensing and speech recognition are producing new levels of functionality for tasks that have only recently been considered practical for robots.

Autonomous unmanned vehicles have sensors and AI software that allow them to act independently rather than being remotely controlled by a human operator. They have a huge potential to work in environments that are dangerous for humans, such as deep-sea exploration, outer space and war zones. There are enormous ethical questions to be answered about the use of vehicles that act independently as a weapon of war.

Increasing Use of Expert Systems

An expert system is a computer program that contains a knowledge base on a particular subject to offer advice or make decisions. Expert systems can save money by removing the need to pay for a human expert.

Contemporary uses of expert systems are in areas such as medicine, helpdesk systems, machine repair and financial decisions.

Expert systems can be used to spot credit-card fraud by comparing a sudden change in the pattern of a card's use compared to previous transactions logged in a database.

ONLINE

Follow the link at www. brightredbooks.net for more information and a demonstration of an expert system working.

ONLINE SYSTEMS

There are hundreds of millions of websites on the World-Wide Web. There is a trend towards an increase in speed and storage capacity of computer networks as a response to storing and transmitting the vast amount of multimedia data contained in these websites.

A particular area of rapid expansion is the number of users of social-media websites. Online shopping is having an increasing impact on the way in which people shop, and is reducing prices by increasing competition and the recycling of second-hand goods.

ONLINE

Keep up to date with latest technology developments by watching 'Click' at www. brightredbooks.net

 ## THINGS TO DO AND THINK ABOUT

When investigating and reporting on a trend in technological development, you should be able to explain why it has come about, how it has developed from older technologies and how it may develop in the future. You should also be able to report on its positive and/or negative impact on the environment, economy and society.

ONLINE TEST

Test yourself on this topic online at www. brightredbooks.net

OUTCOMES AND UNIT ASSESSMENT

ONLINE

You can find more information on the unit assessments for Computing Science at Higher level on the Scottish Qualifications Authority website at www. brightredbooks.net

INTRODUCTION

Each of the two mandatory units (Software Design and Development, Information System Design and Development) requires you to achieve an assessment standard in a set of **learning outcomes**.

In the Software Design and Development unit, there are **three** learning outcomes.

These are listed below.

DON'T FORGET

The learning outcomes are not part of the course assessment. They are a checklist of skills that you have to achieve to pass the unit assessment, but they are not part of the marks that determine your overall grade for the course. It is your marks in the external exam and in the assignment for the course assessment that determine your grade.

OUTCOMES

Outcome 1

Explain how programs work, drawing on an understanding of advanced concepts in software development and computer architecture.

Outcome 2

Develop modular programs using one or more software-development environments.

Outcome 3

Produce a detailed report on the impact of contemporary computing technologies.

DETAILS OF THE OUTCOMES

Each of the three learning outcomes has several parts. All of the subsections must be achieved to gain a pass for the outcome.

Outcome 1

This is a written outcome in which you have to show an understanding of how a program works by explaining parts of its code.

There are four subsections to this outcome:

1.1 Reading and explaining code
1.2 Describing the purpose of a range of programming constructs and how they work
1.3 Describing how a range of standard algorithms work
1.4 Describing how programs relate to low-level structures and operations.

The range of programming constructs should include subprograms, parameters and pre-defined functions. The range of standard algorithms should include input validation, linear search, finding minimum and maximum and counting occurrences.

Outcome 2

This is a practical outcome in which you have to develop modular programs using one or more software-development environments to implement a range of programming constructs. You also have to test your solutions and correct any errors.

contd

There are six subsections to this outcome:

2.1   Applying contemporary design and development methodologies
2.2   Selecting and using combinations of appropriate constructs
2.3   Selecting and using appropriate simple and structured data types, including 1-D arrays
2.4   Testing digital solutions systematically
2.5   Identifying and rectifying program errors
2.6   Applying aspects of good programming technique, including meaningful variable names, internal commentary, indentation.

Structure diagrams and pseudocode can be used to design the program.

The programs must use at least two data types, including 1-D arrays.

The programs should be modular, with the use of subprograms that pass parameters.

You should construct a test plan and then provide evidence of your solution being tested against your plan.

Outcome 3

This is an outcome in which you have to produce a detailed report on the impact of contemporary computing technologies by analysing and evaluating.

There are three subsections to this outcome:

3.1   Current trends in software-development languages and environments
3.2   Current trends in the development of intelligent systems
3.3   Current trends in online systems.

You can choose the software-development language and environment, intelligent system and online system from contemporary applications, games or mobile application-development environments. Either you can choose to report on trends from areas that you have studied in class, or you can investigate a new area by yourself.

You must do an analysis of:

- how each trend builds on previous technologies
- the current stage of development
- and possible future development.

This will also include an evaluation of the social, economic and environmental impacts of the trend.

DON'T FORGET

Make sure in your solutions that you use functions and procedures appropriately. A **function** is used when the subprogram returns a single item of data, and a **procedure** is used to produce an effect. For example, a function would be used to return a maximum value, and a procedure would be used to enter three valid numbers.

DON'T FORGET

You must report on current **trends** in these three areas of computing, and not simply give a description of a software-development language and environment, intelligent system and so on.

EVIDENCE

The evidence you are asked to provide for Outcome 1 may be oral or written.

Evidence for Outcome 2 may be obtained from a single, extended software-development task or from a number of shorter tasks. You are not expected to provide a complete documentation of the program solution; just the criteria outlined in the task.

The report for Outcome 3 should be in a form that can be presented to others. This does not need to be written, but may be reported in some other format, such as a presentation or a website.

THINGS TO DO AND THINK ABOUT

The tasks you are given for unit assessment will depend on your school. Your school may use the SQA assessments, adapt them or make up their own assessment tasks. This is because each school will not use exactly the same software to teach this unit and will therefore have a different approach to learning and assessment. In any case, the assessments that you sit are verified by the SQA to make sure that all students are assessed at the same standard and meet the learning outcomes.

REVISION QUESTIONS 1

QUESTION 1

Standards have been developed for representing numbers, text and graphics in binary in computer systems.

(a) Why do standards exist for the storage of data on computer systems?

(b) What is the largest whole number that can be stored as a 32-bit positive integer?

(c) A programmer is writing a program to process the 100-metre event at the Olympics.

The program needs to store the athletes' times to 2 decimal places.

The programmer is using a language that has two floating-point data types, called 'Real' and 'Surreal'.

'Real' has an 8-bit mantissa and an 8-bit exponent.

'Surreal' has a 24-bit mantissa and a 16-bit exponent.

State whether the 'Real' or 'Surreal' data type is better suited for storing the times, and justify your answer.

(d) ASCII and Unicode are standards for representing text in a computer system.

Give one advantage that each standard has over the other.

(e) Explain how the image shown here would be stored in vector graphics.

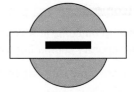

DON'T FORGET

Make sure that you include any working in questions that require calculations. You can still gain some of the marks for correct steps even if your final answer is wrong.

ONLINE

Head to www.brightredbooks.net for the answers to these questions.

QUESTION 2

A catalogue is to be produced for a mail-order company that makes garden gnomes. Each of 80 pages will contain 6 photographs of gnomes. All the pictures will be 2" × 1·5" in 16-bit colour and 600 dpi.

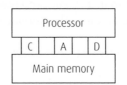

(a) Calculate the storage requirements of 1 photograph in megabytes.

(Give your answer to 1 decimal place.)

(b) Suggest a suitable portable storage device that could be used to hold the entire collection of photographs required for the catalogue, and justify your answer.

(c) A sample of the photographs has to be sent to the company director as e-mail attachments.

Name a utility program that could be used in this situation, and explain why it is useful.

(d) The director is not pleased with the quality of the photographs, and asks for the photographs to be retaken in true colour. What effect would this have on the storage requirements for the photographs?

QUESTION 3

This diagram shows the simplified structure of a desktop computer.
C, A and D represent the three processor buses.

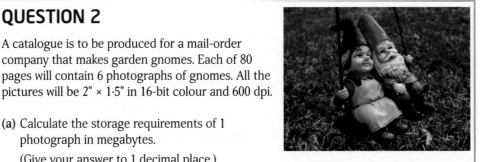

C = Control bus
A = Address bus (32 bits)
D = Data bus (32 bits)

(a) Describe the step involved when the processor fetches and executes an instruction held in main memory.

(Your answer should refer to the role of processor buses and registers.)

(b) (i) Calculate the memory capacity that is potentially addressable by this processor.

(ii) Give two reasons why all the addressable memory might not be installed.

(c) Modern processors use cache to improve their performance. Explain how cache improves processor performance.

QUESTION 4

A program has been written to process scores by the competitors in an ice-skating competition.

Each skater receives a score in the range 0·0–6·0 from each of 6 judges.

A skater's overall score is calculated from the total of the 6 scores minus the best and the worst scores.

Judge	1	2	3	4	5	6
Score	5·2	5·5	4·9	5·2	5·7	5·3

Overall score = 5·2 + 5·5 + 4·9 + 5·2 + 5·7 + 5·3 − 5·7 − 4·9 = 21·2.

(a) The program validates each score entered by the judges with a conditional loop.

Explain why a conditional loop is required.

(b) A subroutine called 'final_score' calculates the overall score for a skater from the 6 judges' scores.

State whether the 'final_score' subroutine is a procedure or a function, and justify your answer.

(c) The 'final_score' subroutine uses an array called 'Scores' as an input parameter.

(i) Explain why an integer data type is not suitable for this parameter, and give a suitable data type.

(ii) State whether the 'Scores' array should be passed by reference or by value, and explain your answer.

(d) This program could have used 6 separate variables or a 1-dimensional array to store the judges' scores for an ice-skater.

What are the advantages of a 1-dimensional array over 6 variables in terms of:

(i) future maintenance;

(ii) efficiency;

(iii) data storage requirements?

(e) The pseudocode alongside shows an algorithm to calculate the overall score, but has three incomplete lines.

Complete the pseudocode for line 12, line 18 and line 20 of the algorithm.

```
1   SET Scores TO [5·2, 5·5, 4·9, 5·2, 5·7, 5·3]
2   SET Position TO 0
3   SET Min TO Scores(Position)
4   FOR Position FROM 1 TO 5 DO
5       IF Scores(Position) < Min THEN
6           SET Min TO Scores(Position)
7       END IF
8   END FOR
9   SET Position TO 0
10  SET Max TO Scores(Position)
11  FOR Position FROM 1 TO 5 DO
12      IF ...
13          SET Max TO Scores(Position)
14      END IF
15  END FOR
16  SET Total TO 0
17  FOR Position FROM 0 TO 5 DO
18      SET Total TO ...
19  END FOR
20  SET Overall TO ...
21  SEND ["The overall score is: ", Overall] TO DISPLAY
```

 THINGS TO DO AND THINK ABOUT

Any questions involving pseudocode will be set with the SQA's standardised pseudocode notation. You should be familiar with the format of the pseudocode instructions from the National 5 course.

 DON'T FORGET

Don't be too vague with the language you use in your answers. Make sure that you use any relevant technical terms and explain/describe with precise and detailed sentences.

REVISION QUESTIONS 2

QUESTION 1

The Chicago Cab Company has a fleet of 40 taxis. The director has decided to use a software-development company to computerise the business.

The first phase of the development process is for a systems analyst to identify the requirements of the system.

(a) Describe **two** techniques the systems analyst can use to extract information on the client's needs.

(b) A new printer is to be bought for the network.

State **two** technical factors that should be considered when choosing a printer.

(c) (i) The software used a rapid application development methodology to produce the system.

Describe **two** techniques that are used in rapid application development.

(ii) Explain why rapid application development would not be suitable for creating a system to control the fuel rods in a nuclear power station.

(d) Once the software-development company has completed and tested the program, it is delivered for beta testing.

Explain why beta testing is necessary when the software-development team has already tested the completed program.

(e) At some point in the future, most computer systems require maintenance.

Why would the client need to pay for perfective and adaptive maintenance but not for corrective maintenance?

ONLINE

Head to www.
brightredbooks.net for the
answers to these questions.

DON'T FORGET

It is a common mistake, when asked to supply sets of test data, just to say 'normal, extreme and exhaustive'. You must give actual examples of test data that is to be entered into the program. In this question, you must give six actual numbers for each set of test data.

QUESTION 2

Testing of software can never show that the software is error-free, but it should be as comprehensive as possible given time and money constraints. Often, independent test groups are brought in to test the programs.

(a) Why do software-development companies employ independent test groups to test software, rather than let the software be tested by the programmers who wrote it?

(b) A program subroutine enters six test scores in the range 0...25 and calculates the number of fails (0...12), passes (13...22) and passes with distinction (23...25).

The subroutine should validate the scores in the range 0...25.

Give three sets of test data that could be used to test this subroutine fully, giving a reason why you have chosen each set of test data.

(c) For each set of test data, give the expected output from the subroutine.

QUESTION 3

An integrated package has word-processing, spreadsheet, database and graphics sections. The package has a built-in scripting language and macro facility.

(a) Explain what is meant by a scripting language.

(b) A certain user of the integrated package always puts his name as a header and the date as a footer on all his documents.

Describe an efficient method of adding the header and footer to the documents.

(c) Programs in the field of artificial intelligence are created using declarative languages.

Describe two features of a declarative language.

(d) Some languages have both an interpreted and a compiled version. Explain what advantage having both versions will have on:

  (i) the speed of development of the software

  (ii) the storage requirements and speed of execution of the final software.

QUESTION 4

A program is used to enter and process the results of a cross-country running competition. The program enters the name, sex, year group, age and finishing time of each competitor.

The program stores the details for 80 competitors using different data types.

(a) (i) Explain the term 'data type'.

  (ii) What data structure and data type would be used within the program to store the names of the 80 competitors?

(b) Four standard algorithms are:

  1   linear search

  2   counting occurrences

  3   finding maximum

  4   finding minimum.

  Which standard algorithms would the program use to find:

  (i) the number of girls in the race

  (ii) the best time for the race?

(c) On the day of the race, the finishing times of the 80 competitors are entered into the program.

An athlete who runs the race in less than 12 minutes gains a star award.

Using a design notation with which you are familiar, write an algorithm which would find the number of athletes who gained a star award.

(d) The program was designed with a high level of modular independence.

  (i) Explain how the use of local and global variables impacts on modular independence.

  (ii) Describe one benefit of developing software with independent modules.

 THINGS TO DO AND THINK ABOUT

The new course has an emphasis on problem-solving rather than memorising facts, but you still need to learn the theory covered in this book before you can apply it to solve problems.

 **DON'T FORGET**

When answering questions, it is important that your handwriting is reasonably neat. It does not need to be a work of art, but it is difficult to gain marks if the marker can't read your answer!

INFORMATION SYSTEM DESIGN AND DEVELOPMENT

DATABASES 1

DON'T FORGET

A primary key is used to uniquely identify each record in the table. In this case, the 'Dwarf ID' field is the primary key. Using a field such as 'Name' as a primary key would not always work, since more than one person could have the same name. A compound key is a type of primary key which uses a combination of two or more fields to uniquely identify a record.

DATABASE STRUCTURE

A database is an organised collection of records holding data so that it can be stored, amended and accessed quickly. Databases are an essential part of the computer system in organisations such as banks, schools, sports clubs, e-commerce companies and so on, which store and process data on customers, products, orders and so on.

A relational database stores data in several linked tables. The main advantages of relating tables are improved accuracy and less duplication of data, since data is entered only once, and fewer errors result.

Shown below is a database table storing records on the Seven Dwarfs.

Each row in the table represents a record, which is the data values held on one dwarf.

Each column in the table represents a field, which is one item of data in a record, such as a postcode.

Field

Dwarfs table

Dwarf ID	Name	Age	Street	Town	Postcode	Married
1	Sneezy	288	3 Uncut Drive	Diamond City	D12 9TH	Yes
2	Sleepy	250	20 White Street	Whitehaven	WH3 8UH	Yes
3	Happy	60	15 Mine Terrace	Disneyville	D33 7TB	No
4	Grumpy	501	120 HiHo Avenue	Minehead	M55 1WQ	Yes
5	Dopey	16	33 Disney Boulevard	Queenstown	Q2 5SW	No
6	Bashful	12	14 Snow Crescent	Diamond City	D12 3DT	No
7	Doc	199	222 Queen Street	Disneyville	D80 3FT	Yes

Record → (row 5)

ONE-TO-ONE RELATIONSHIP

Example:

This example uses the Dwarfs table to illustrate a one-to-one relationship between tables.

A one-to-one relationship can be used to split a large table into two smaller tables. In this example, the Dwarfs table is split into a Dwarf table and a Dwarf Address table, with the two tables linked with the Dwarf ID field.

The term **one-to-one** refers to the fact that one record in the Dwarf table is linked to one record in the Dwarf Address table.

Dwarf table

Dwarf ID	Name	Age	Married
1	Sneezy	288	Yes
2	Sleepy	250	Yes
3	Happy	60	No
4	Grumpy	501	Yes
5	Dopey	16	No
6	Bashful	12	No
7	Doc	199	Yes

Dwarf Address table

Dwarf ID	Street	Town	Postcode
1	3 Uncut Drive	Diamond City	D12 9TH
2	20 White Street	Whitehaven	WH3 8UH
3	15 Mine Terrace	Disneyville	D33 7TB
4	120 HiHo Avenue	Minehead	M55 1WQ
5	33 Disney Boulevard	Queenstown	Q2 5SW
6	14 Snow Crescent	Diamond City	D12 3DT
7	222 Queen Street	Disneyville	D80 3FT

contd

An Entity Relationship Diagram is a method of design used to illustrate the types of relationships between tables in a relational database. The one-to-one relationship is illustrated in the Entity Relationship Diagram shown here.

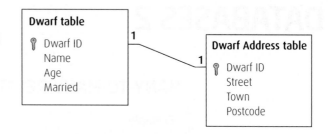

Dwarf table
- Dwarf ID
- Name
- Age
- Married

Dwarf Address table
- Dwarf ID
- Street
- Town
- Postcode

ONE-TO-MANY RELATIONSHIP

Example:

This example uses the Dwarfs table and another two tables named Products and Orders to illustrate a one-to-many relationship between tables.

The Seven Dwarfs order items such as pickaxes and hats, which are stored in a Products table.

Each product has a primary key named 'Product ID' and other details about the product.

When a dwarf orders a product, it is stored as a record in an Orders table.

Each order has a primary key named 'Order ID' to uniquely identify the order, and a field to store the date of the order. The 'Dwarf ID' and 'Product ID' fields are used to link the Orders table to the Dwarfs and Products tables respectively by placing their key field in the Orders table.

These key fields are called foreign keys in the Orders table, since they have travelled abroad to another table.

This saves the need to duplicate all of the field data for the dwarfs and the products in the Orders table, since only the primary key is required in the Orders table to link to the other data in the Dwarfs and Products tables.

The Dwarfs table and the Products tables are both linked to the Orders table in a one-to-many relationship.

The term **one-to-many** refers to the fact that one record in the Dwarfs table can appear in many records in the Orders table. Also, one record in the Products table can appear in many records in the Orders table.

Products table

Product ID	Article	Price (£)	Quantity	Supplier
1	Small pickaxe	79·99	9	MiningLand
2	Medium pickaxe	134·99	217	MiningLand
3	Large pickaxe	199·00	5	MiningLand
4	Soft hat (red)	24·99	80	The Headgear Company
5	Soft hat (blue)	24·99	80	The Headgear Company
6	Beard shampoo	2·95	56	Boots

Orders table

Order ID	Date	Dwarf ID	Product ID
1	12/05/2014	2	4
2	23/05/2014	2	6
3	02/06/2014	6	3
4	02/06/2014	1	3
5	25/06/2014	5	5
6	28/06/2014	7	3
7	07/07/2014	7	4
8	10/07/2014	2	2
9	20/07/2014	3	4
10	24/07/2014	4	1

The links between the tables are illustrated in the Entity Relationship Diagram below, where 'many' is represented by the infinity symbol ∞.

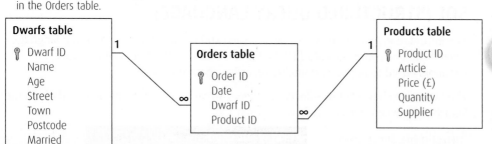

Dwarfs table
- Dwarf ID
- Name
- Age
- Street
- Town
- Postcode
- Married

Orders table
- Order ID
- Date
- Dwarf ID
- Product ID

Products table
- Product ID
- Article
- Price (£)
- Quantity
- Supplier

 ONLINE

Have a look at Microsoft help pages for further explanations of database uses at www.brightredbooks.net

 ONLINE TEST

How well have you learned this topic? Take the test at www.brightredbooks.net

THINGS TO DO AND THINK ABOUT

When creating a relational database, the design of the tables and the types of relationship between the tables have consequences for the queries and reports that will be performed. In your practical work, sketch out a design of the tables and their relationships before you implement your database solution on the computer.

DATABASES 2

MANY-TO-MANY RELATIONSHIP

Example:

This example uses the Dwarfs table and another table named Courses to illustrate a many-to-many relationship between tables. The dwarfs go on training courses for diamond-cutting, pickaxe skills, mine-tunnelling and so on, which are held in records in a Courses table.

Courses table				
Course ID	Description	Fee (£)	Duration (days)	Educational Institution
1	Diamond-cutting	160·00	2	Diamond Street College
2	Elementary pickaxe skills	120·00	2	Minehead College
3	Mine-tunnelling	170·00	3	Minehead College
4	Diamond-polishing	85·00	1	Diamond Street College
5	Advanced pickaxe skills	135·00	3	Minehead College
6	Choir singing	110·00	1	The Music Institute
7	People management	90·00	2	Modern Business College

The Dwarfs table and the Courses table are linked in a **many-to-many relationship**.

This is a many-to-many relationship because one record in the Dwarfs table can appear in many records in the Courses table. Also, one record in the Courses table can be linked to many records in the Dwarfs table.

In other words, a dwarf can do more than one course, and a course can be taken by more than one dwarf.

Many-to-many relationships are considered to be confusing and a poor relational database design. For this reason, many-to-many relationships are replaced with two one-to-many relationships using a **join table** between the two tables. In this case, the Signup table is the join table, which has its own primary key; and the Dwarf ID and Course ID fields are foreign keys which link the tables.

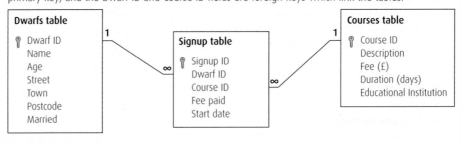

ONLINE

Visit www.brightredbooks. net and try out the SQL tutorials.

DON'T FORGET

There are three types of relationships between tables in a relational database which you will cover in your practical work in this course. These are one-to-one, one-to-many and many-to-many.

SQL (STRUCTURED QUERY LANGUAGE)

The information in a database can be accessed and modified using a scripting language called SQL. The commands SELECT, WHERE, INSERT, UPDATE and DELETE are commonly used to access and modify records in database tables.

The SQL code shown below selects the Name, Street and Town fields of records from the Dwarfs table where the Age field is less than 100.

```
SELECT Name, Street, Town
FROM Dwarfs
WHERE Age<100;
```

Result of SQL script		
Name	Street	Town
Happy	15 Mine Terrace	Disneyville
Dopey	33 Disney Boulevard	Queenstown
Bashful	14 Snow Crescent	Diamond City

contd

SQL is commonly used for managing web-based databases. The content of web pages that are based on information in a database can be dynamically updated using SQL code. For example, stock levels in an e-commerce web page can be updated each time the web page loads.

COMPLEX DATABASE OPERATIONS

Queries

Queries are used to interrogate a database in order to retrieve specific information. For example, a query could be used to select orders that have been placed in the last three months, or to select dwarfs over the age of 100 who have ordered a large pickaxe.

Forms

A form is used to make it easier to enter data by providing a screen layout that only contains the necessary fields. Displaying the records in columns can also make it easier for the data to be entered by working down a column rather than scrolling through complete records.

Reports

A database report presents information based on a table or query in an attractive manner. A report can sort the records in a specific way, display only certain fields, provide summaries of information and so on.

Example:

A report could be created to display information on the Dwarfs who have ordered large pickaxes.

First of all, a query can be created with the following fields:

```
Order.Product ID and criteria = 3
Product.Article
Dwarf.Name
Order.Date
Order.Supplier
```

A report can then be created using the data from the query.

Product ID: 3			
Article	**Name**	**Date**	**Supplier**
Large pickaxe	Sneezy	02/06/2014	MiningLand
Large pickaxe	Bashful	02/06/2014	MiningLand
Large pickaxe	Doc	28/06/2014	MiningLand

DATA DICTIONARY

A data dictionary is a file that defines the basic organisation of a database. It contains a list of all tables in the database, the number of records in each table, and the names and types of each field. Most database systems keep the data dictionary hidden from users to prevent them from accidentally destroying its contents. Data dictionaries contain information for managing the database but not the actual data itself.

 THINGS TO DO AND THINK ABOUT

You will use a database program in your practical work. Ask your teacher to demonstrate the features provided with this software to create queries, forms and reports.

 ONLINE TEST

How well have you learned this topic? Take the test at www.brightredbooks.net

WEBSITES

WEB-PAGE STRUCTURE

HTML is a language used to create web pages. The language uses tags to describe the elements of the page, such as a head, title, body, style, font size and so on.

The basic format of a tag is of the form: <TAG> text </TAG> .

For example: <title> BBC – Homepage </title>

Example:

This example shows how tags are used to create a simple HTML document:

```
<html>
<head>
    <title> Higher Computing </title>
</head>
<body>
    <h1> Welcome to the course </h1>
    <p> This text is in normal style </p>
    <p> <b> This text is in bold style </b></p>
    <p> <u> This text is in underlined style </u> </p>
    <p> <i> This text is in italic style </i> </p>
    <p align = "center"> This text is centre-aligned </p>
</body>
</html>
```

The <html> tags are placed around the whole file to identify it as an HTML file.
The <head> tag is used at the start of the file to define details such as the title of the page, which is defined in the <title> tag.
The <title> tag is included in the head part of the document. The text you put here is what shows up in the title bar at the top of the browser.
The <body> tag starts after the head tag and ends just before the last HTML tag. It is placed around the main content of the page.
The <h1> (headline size 1), <p> (new paragraph), <b> (bold), <u> (underline) and <i> (italic) tags are used to format text.
<p align = "center"> is used to centre-align the paragraph text.

Hyperlinks

A hyperlink is implemented by specifying the URL of the website and the text to be used to activate the link.

Example:

<p><a href="http://www.jazzwise.com//">Jazz</a></p>

Metatags

These tags are put into a web page to provide information about a page that is then used by search engines.

The **keywords** metatag is used to list words which describe the content of the page. The **description** metatag is used to give the text of the summary displayed when the page appears in the results of a search engine.

Example:

<meta name="keywords" content="open, open championship, golf, golfcourses"></meta>
<meta name="description" content="The Open Championship Official Website."></meta>

CSS

CSS is short for Cascading Style Sheets. It uses style sheets to define the formatting of elements of a web page, such as headers and hyperlinks, by defining colour, font, text alignment, size, borders, table sizes and so on. Once a style-sheet file has been created, the formatting can be used by web pages that reference that style sheet.

It makes it easier to have consistent formatting in all of the pages of a website, since a style sheet has to be created only once and then can be used by any page that references the CSS file. It also means that any changes to the formatting on the style sheet will automatically apply to all of the web pages that reference the style sheet.

contd

Cascading Style Sheets follow the syntax of: Identifier {property: value}

Example:

```
<html>

<head>
<style>
body
{
background-color: blue;
font-weight: bold;
}
H1
{
font-family: "Comic Sans MS";
font-size: 36px;
color: yellow;
text-align: center;
}
H2
{
font-family: "Times New Roman";
font-size: 12px;
color: white;
}
</style>
</head>

<body>
<H1>MAIN HEADING</H1>
<H2>Subheading.</H2>
</body>

</html>
```

In this question, the HTML tag of a main heading H1 is used as an identifier which includes a list of style statements, which is then followed by a subheading identifier H2 and its formatting rules.

The text-formatting rules are declared in the <head> tag and are then used in the <body> tag.

This code would result in the display shown below.

MAIN HEADING
Subheading.

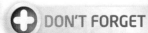 **DON'T FORGET**

The term **cascading** is used to describe the fact that changes to a style sheet will cascade through to all of the web pages that are based on that style sheet.

ONLINE

Visit www.brightredbooks. net and try out the HTML and CSS tutorials.

 ONLINE

Visit www.brightredbooks. net for a glossary of web terminology.

MORE WEB-PAGE CONCEPTS

Dynamic Web Page

Some websites have their content linked to a database. If the contents of the database are changed, then the website is automatically updated at the same time. For example, a website used for e-commerce will have items of stock and their quantity stored in a database. When an item is purchased, the quantity field in the database for that item will be reduced by 1, which will be updated in the quantity displayed on the website.

Database-driven Website

Database-driven websites like this use the scripting language SQL (Structured Query Language) to link the database content to the website.

Interactive Web Page

An interactive web page is one that provides interaction with the user – for example, clicking on a forward arrow to play a video, clicking on a button to initiate an event, playing music and so on.

Multimedia Application

Many websites contain sound and video as well as text and images. A multimedia application is one that includes a combination of text, audio, images and video in an interactive environment.

Multi-level Navigation

A simple website with a small number of pages can be navigated at one level by providing links from each page to each of the other pages. However, in a more complex website with a large number of web pages, multi-level navigation is needed in which the user navigates through a hierarchy of sections and subsections.

 ONLINE TEST

Head to www. brightredbooks.net and take the 'Websites' test.

 ## THINGS TO DO AND THINK ABOUT

Visit the BBC website at www.bbc.co.uk, which has links to News, Sport, Weather and so on. Each of these sections links through to submenus of web pages.

Think about how you can use multi-level navigation between different sections and subsections on this site.

USER INTERFACE

TERMS DESCRIBING SOFTWARE

There are various terms that are used to describe and evaluate computer software. These include **usability**, **fit for purpose**, **efficient**, **robust** and **maintainable**.

Usability

The term **usability** describes how intuitive and user-friendly the software is to use. For example, menus and toolbars should have their options in places where you would expect to find them.

For example, it should not take a long time to learn how to use the home page of a website. It should only take a few seconds for a user to take in the functions available on the page.

Fit for Purpose

Software is **fit for purpose** if the product is suitable for its intended purpose – that is, if it does what it is supposed to do in terms of the software specification.

Efficient

It is not **efficient** to solve a small problem with a very large program. Also, the speed of execution of a program can vary considerably depending on the design, code and language in which it is written. A program which runs very slowly is not efficient.

The use of arrays, and then processing the array values in loops, is much more efficient than using many individual variables that each need to be assigned a value in separate instructions.

> **DON'T FORGET**
>
> Software is said to be efficient if its time or storage requirements are in proportion to the scale of the problem.

Example:

Two programs each enter seven numbers and then calculate and display the average number.

Program A uses an array, which makes the program more efficient than Program B, which does not use an array.

Program A

```
1   SET Total TO 0
2   FOR Position FROM 0 TO 6 DO
3       RECEIVE List_of_numbers(Position) FROM KEYBOARD
4       SET Total TO Total + List_of_numbers(Position)
5   END FOR
6   SEND ["The average is: ", Total/7] TO DISPLAY
```

Program B

```
1   SET Total TO 0
2   RECEIVE Number1 FROM KEYBOARD
3   SET Total TO Total + Number1
4   RECEIVE Number2 FROM KEYBOARD
5   SET Total TO Total + Number2
6   RECEIVE Number3 FROM KEYBOARD
7   SET Total TO Total + Number3
8   RECEIVE Number4 FROM KEYBOARD
9   SET Total TO Total + Number4
10  RECEIVE Number5 FROM KEYBOARD
11  SET Total TO Total + Number5
12  RECEIVE Number6 FROM KEYBOARD
13  SET Total TO Total + Number6
14  RECEIVE Number7 FROM KEYBOARD
15  SET Total TO Total + Number7
16  SEND ["The average is: ", Total/7] TO DISPLAY
```

contd

Robust

Software is **robust** if it does not crash easily with unexpected input. For example, if the user enters a letter when numeric data is expected, the software should not just crash but should give an error message and invite the user to re-enter the data.

Maintainable

Software is **maintainable** if subsequent modifications can be performed easily and quickly to adapt to different circumstances.

ACCESSIBILITY

The **accessibility** of software is a term that describes how effectively it can be used by users with certain kinds of disabilities. Most software producers take steps to ensure that the software can be used by people with or without disabilities.

- **Physical disabilities that prevent the user from holding or controlling a mouse.**

  Most operating systems allow the settings for the mouse to be changed. For example, the response time of a double click can be changed to a slower speed for people who find it hard to click fast; or the pointer can be made larger for people with poor eyesight.

  Keyboard navigation can also be used as an alternative means of interacting with the menus and buttons of a graphical user interface without using a mouse.

- **Physical disabilities that prevent the user from typing or from using a keyboard.**

  Voice-recognition software can be used as an alternative to typing on a keyboard. This software can also help people with spelling difficulties, such as users with dyslexia, since recognised words are almost always correctly spelled.

- **Users with poor vision.**

  Zooming in on a high-contrast display can help users who have this type of disability. Also, settings can be made available for increasing the sizes of fonts and icons.

- **Colour-blind users.**

  For colour-blind users, the display must be presented in a form that uses a carefully selected combination of colours. The display must avoid combinations of colours that would be indistinguishable to a colour-blind user.

- **Blind users.**

  Voice recognition can be used for input; or Braille keyboards can be used which have keys with raised dots that can be read with the fingers by blind people.

  Instead of a visual display, an application called a screen reader can be used to read sections of the screen aloud.

ONLINE

Head to www. brightredbooks.net for information on accessibility features provided by Google in their products.

ONLINE TEST

Test yourself on this topic online at www. brightredbooks.net

OPTIMISATION

Software may be **optimised** so that it executes faster or operates with fewer resources. A program may be optimised to work efficiently with the available resources such as memory, the display size or power.

Multi-core processors execute programs differently from single-core processors, therefore producing different versions of the same code for different processors is sometimes required to optimise the performance.

Different versions of a website are displayed, when it is downloaded to a smartphone versus a desktop computer, to optimise the display for the size of screen.

 THINGS TO DO AND THINK ABOUT

The BBC website (www.bbc.co.uk) is optimised when viewed on a browser overseas, in the sense that the content and the language used in the articles are different. The next time that you are overseas, have a look at the BBC website in that country.

MEDIA TYPES

ONLINE

Head to www.
brightredbooks.net to
find out more about file
compression.

FILE COMPRESSION

File compression is used to reduce the size of a file.

Lossy compression is a technique that results in **some** of the detail being lost in the compressed file.

Lossless compression is a technique that results in **none** of the detail being lost in the compressed file.

SOUND

MP3 is a file format that is widely used for storing music sound files.

This is a **lossy** file-compression format which has a high compression factor – and this, coupled with little loss of quality, has resulted in its widespread commercial use.

The compression works by:
1   removing sounds that are inaudible to the human ear
2   when two similar sounds occur at the same time, the quieter sound is removed.

GRAPHICS

Compression techniques used with graphics files include RLE (Run Length Encoding), LZW (Lempel Ziv Welch) and CLUT (Colour Look-up Table).

- **RLE** – Often, a bit-mapped graphic has areas where the same-coloured pixel is repeated many times. This compression technique stores the colour code for 1 pixel and for how many times it is repeated, instead of the same code for individual pixels over and over again. This can reduce the file size considerably if a large area is the same colour, but not so much if the whole image is very varied.

  RLE will compress Image 1 much more than Image 2 because it has repeated pixels which are the same colour.

Image 1

- **LZW** – This compression technique looks for commonly repeated patterns of bits that are stored in a look-up table. Each pattern is allocated an index number, so that the index number can be stored rather than the patterns.

- **CLUT** – This is a facility that enables a subset of colours to be stored as a local palette. For example, an 8-bit code would give a CLUT with 256 colours, which could be selected from a full 24-bit colour range.

- **Bitmap** – 24-bit bit-mapped graphics give true colour with 2^{24} colours but are heavy on storage requirements. RLE and LZW compression can be used to reduce the file size.

Image 2

- **GIF (Graphics Interchange Format)** – GIF uses LZW lossless compression. Each pixel is represented in 8 bits, which allows for 256 colours.

  GIFs have a transparency feature where a specific colour can be made transparent so that parts of an image do not obscure the one behind.

- **PNG (Portable Network Graphics)** – This is a **lossless** file format intended to replace GIF by adding extra features.

  The PNG file format has a higher compression factor than GIF files and also has a transparency feature, but in addition it has an opaqueness attribute that allows the degree of transparency of pixels to be set.

contd

- **JPEG (Joint Photographic Expert Group)** – This file format uses lossy compression. The loss in detail can range from being barely noticeable to seriously reducing the quality of the image.

VIDEO

- **Compression Techniques** – Compression techniques used with video files include **intraframe** and **interframe** compression.

  Intraframe compression compresses each individual frame typically into lossy JPEG format.

  Interframe compression does not store all of the frames. Instead, it stores key frames (typically every 10th to 15th frame) and then stores only the changes compared to the key frame in subsequent frames.

- **Animated GIFs** – Animated GIFs create apparent movement by showing a sequence of still frames. A rate of around 20 frames per second is needed to produce reasonably fluent motion, therefore file sizes can be large. LZW compression is commonly used to reduce the file size.

- **AVI (Audio Video Interleave)** – This video file format supports a maximum frame rate of 30 frames per second and a resolution of 320 x 240 pixels per frame. AVI files do not have built-in compression.

- **MPEG (Motion Picture Experts Group)** – This format is the standard file format for DVDs, mainly because it has a high compression ratio. This file format stores a few key frames as compressed JPEGs. Subsequent frames after a key frame are compared to the key frame, and only the changes are saved.

ONLINE

Find out more about other video file formats, such as MOV and DV (Digital Video), using the internet.

CALCULATION OF SOUND AND VIDEO FILE SIZES

Calculation of Sound Files

File size = [Time in seconds] × [Sampling rate] × [Sample size] × [Number of channels].

Example:

Calculate the file size of a 7-minute audio clip recorded in stereo with a sample frequency of 44·1 KHz and a sample depth of 24 bits.
File size = 420 × 44,100 × 24 bits × 2 = 889,056,000 bits = 111,132,000 bytes = 106 Mb.

Calculation of Video Files

File size = [Time in seconds] × [Frames per second] × [Number of pixels in one frame] × [Bit depth].

Example:

Calculate the uncompressed file size of a 37-second video clip, captured at 20 frames per second with a resolution of 320 × 240 and 24-bit colour.
File size
= 37 × 20 × 320 × 240 × 24 = 1,363,968,000 bits = 170,496,000 bytes = 163 Mb.

DON'T FORGET

Mono sound has one channel, and stereo sound has two channels. Quadraphonic sound is high-quality sound which uses four channels.

THINGS TO DO AND THINK ABOUT

There are two main reasons for compressing a file:

1 Less storage space is required for the compressed file.

2 The compressed file can be transmitted more quickly over a network.

ONLINE TEST

How well have you learned this topic? Take the test at www.brightredbooks.net

CODING

SCRIPTING LANGUAGES

Most programming languages, such as Visual Basic and Python, are used to write an entire program from scratch. The programmer has to declare variables to store the program's data and use the features of the language to input, process and output data.

A **scripting language** is different in that it is a programming language designed to work alongside another program. Examples of scripting languages are JavaScript, which is used in conjunction with HTML (Hypertext Mark-up Language), and VBA (Visual Basic for Applications), which can be used to automate repeated tasks and customise Microsoft Office documents. A language used for writing an entire application is typically compiled before it is run, whereas a scripting language is interpreted from source code one instruction at a time when it is run.

Scripting languages are widely used on the World-Wide Web to increase the functionality of web pages and to make them more interactive and dynamic.

On a **client-server network**, there are two types of computers, called **servers** and **clients**. Server computers such as the file server and the print server provide network resources, and client computers make use of the resources provided by the server.

Scripting languages are classified into **client-side** and **server-side** depending upon whether the client or the server is running the script.

CLIENT-SIDE SCRIPTING LANGUAGES

Client-side scripting languages are the class of scripting languages that are executed on the client computers of a network. Client-side scripts are often part of a document (embedded script), but they may also be contained in a separate file which is referenced by the document that uses it (external script).

When the user requests a web page from the server, the server finds the page and sends it to the user's computer. The page is displayed on the browser, with any client-side scripts running during or after display.

Client-side scripting can be used to provide additional functionality and flexibility to websites and other application programs. HTML is limited in that its main purpose is to describe the text, graphics, video and sound elements of a web page and provide formatting information on its content.

contd

It requires languages such as JavaScript, JScript, VBScript and others to add extra functionality to a website – for example, displaying an image when the mouse hovers over an image, adding animation, validation of the data entered into a form and providing complex menu systems. Client-side scripts may also contain instructions for the browser to execute in response to certain user actions such as clicking a command button or selecting an item from a drop-down list.

Client-side scripting languages can be used in applications other than web pages. For example, VBA could be used to create a keyboard shortcut to automatically put the user's name in a header in a long document. Another example could be to add a command button to a spreadsheet that sorts the data in a table when clicked.

SERVER-SIDE SCRIPTING LANGUAGES

Server-side scripting languages are the class of scripting languages that are executed on the server computers of a network.

When the user requests a web page from the server, the script in the page is interpreted by the server creating or changing the page content to suit the user and the occasion. The page in its final form is sent to the user and then cannot be changed using server-side scripting.

Languages such as Perl, PHP, Java and others are executed by the web server when the user requests a document. They produce output in a form that can be interpreted by web browsers (usually HTML), which is then sent to the user's computer. The script's source code is not seen by the user, who may not be aware that a script was executed.

Server-side scripts are mainly used for managing the site's content by presenting data held in a database which is presented to the user on request. This can be used to improve the security of a website by allowing restricted access to content.

Server-side scripting tends to be used for allowing users to have accounts that are customised to individuals by providing personalised data from databases. E-commerce and social networking sites all rely heavily on server-side scripting.

Sites such as Google, Amazon and Facebook all use both client-side and server-side scripting:

- The server-side scripts handle logging in and provide data which is specific to the user.

- The client-side scripts make the page more interactive by performing actions such as triggering events when a button is pressed, processing data that has been entered into text boxes and so on.

 THINGS TO DO AND THINK ABOUT

Your own school will have a client-server network. Ask your teacher or the network manager how client-side and server-side scripts are managed on the network.

 ONLINE

Investigate JavaScript and server-side scripting languages by following the link at www.brightredbooks.net. This link allows you to work through tutorials on these and various other scripting languages.

 DON'T FORGET

Client-side scripts are interpreted and executed by the browser and therefore depend on the memory and CPU performance of the client computer. Server-side scripts run on the server and depend on the memory and CPU performance of the server.

 ONLINE TEST

Take the test on coding at www.brightredbooks.net

TESTING

INTRODUCTION

The purpose of testing an information system is to identify and rectify errors.

Testing should not be random but should be organised according to a test plan that uses appropriate criteria for the software to be tested against. The test results should be documented with hard copy or electronic evidence.

For a website, testing will include:

- checking that the user-interface design is appropriate for the target user
- checking that all levels of navigation work
- checking that all internal and external hyperlinks work
- checking that text, graphics and videos display properly and that sound files work properly
- checking that scripts work correctly.

BETA TESTING

In the software-development process, a **beta test** is the second phase of software testing, where the clients try out the software in their own workplace. (Beta is the second letter of the Greek alphabet.) Originally, the term **alpha test** meant the first phase of testing in the software-development process, which is carried out by the developers of the software. Beta-test versions of games software are often distributed to gamers on the web to give the program a 'real-world' test and also to provide a preview of the next release.

Beta testing gives the developers an opportunity to gain feedback from the clients on the usability and functionality of the software and to allow modifications to be made before the final version is produced.

USABILITY

Usability testing measures the capacity of target users of an information system to meet its intended purpose.

Users can be asked to perform given tasks under controlled conditions to determine how easy they find it to use the software. For example, users can be asked to navigate around certain pages of a website, and the number of clicks and the time taken can be recorded. Users can also be given post-test questionnaires to provide their feedback on the usability of the software.

TESTING COMPATIBILITY

Compatibility testing is carried out to ensure that an information system works properly in its intended environment. This type of testing is carried out to determine how well a system performs in a particular environment that includes hardware, operating system, web browser and other software.

Hardware

The computers that are to run the information system will have a specification that includes processor, RAM and hard-disc capacity. It is important to do test runs in order to make sure that the hardware is sufficient to run the software efficiently and without crashing.

Software

Operating systems such as Windows are constantly being updated. Software written for a newer version of an operating system may be incompatible with an older version of that operating system if it misses some of the features and functionality that the software depends on. Software that works on older versions of an operating system is said to be **backwards-compatible**.

One issue for a website is to test it in as many browsers as possible. Each browser interprets the coding for a website in a slightly different manner, which means that the website can appear different when displayed in different browsers. The appearance and functionality of the website should be viewed on multiple browsers to make sure that all of the features and functions behave as they are supposed to.

 THINGS TO DO AND THINK ABOUT

For a website that you have created, you can do a form of beta testing by getting other members of your class to try out the features and functions of your website. You may find that the software is not as usable as you thought! It may not be as obvious to other people how to use the software as it is to you, since you created the features and functions. Make up a questionnaire with questions such as 'Was it easy to navigate around the website?', 'Did you receive helpful feedback when you made a mistake?', 'Was the interface consistent and clear?' and so on.

 ONLINE

Read more about software testing at www.brightredbooks.net

 ONLINE TEST

Test yourself on this topic online at www.brightredbooks.net

PURPOSE, FEATURES, FUNCTIONALITY AND USERS

PURPOSE

The developers of an information system must have a clear idea of what it is to be used for. The purpose of an information system is what the software aims to achieve.

For example, the purpose of the BBC weather app is to provide temperature, precipitation and wind details for the next 5 days in locations throughout the world.

The purpose will have a bearing on the system's design in terms of content, user interface and accessibility features.

FEATURES AND FUNCTIONALITY

A **feature** is an object that exists in an information system, such as a command button, text box, image or hyperlink text.

A **function** is an action that can be performed on an object. For example, a video file is an object that has actions such as play, pause, close and so on. Another example of an object is a text box which has functions such as enter text, change font, delete text and so on. The features and functions of an information system will depend on what kind of information system it is. For example, a website, a database or a smartphone app will have different features and functions to suit the software and the device on which it is implemented.

DON'T FORGET

The features and functions of an information system refer to the items that exist in an information system and the functions that these objects can perform.

TYPES OF USER

A website is designed to be used by different types of human users.

An information system must take into account the abilities and experience of the intended users. If it is not user-friendly, then it is not fit for purpose, and the users will end up not using it. The designer of an information system must consider the ability, age and language of the users.

Designing software which allows the user to customise the interface is one way to make the information system suitable to different types of users.

Novice

A novice user will require a graphical user interface with pull-down menus, icons and online help. This means that the novice does not have to remember commands and can find options by exploring the menus and the toolbar icons.

Expert

An expert user can find a graphical interface slow and clumsy to use, since often several mouse-clicks can be required to navigate through layers of menus to access a function. Therefore, an expert user would require access to a more complex and detailed interface with more advanced features such as keyboard shortcuts and the use of a scripting language to create macros.

Age-range

The age of the user has an impact on the design of the interface. A young user will find the interface easier if it has colourful images and small amounts of simple text. Older users may have arthritis, poor eyesight or other problems, and so may require large icons and font size and a clear display.

ONLINE

Go online and look at the home page of the BBC website and the home page of the Children's BBC website. Compare their interfaces in terms of the amount of pictures and the amount of text used in each web page.

CRAWLERS AND BOTS

Crawlers

Crawlers are programs that automatically 'crawl' around the web searching for pages to include in search-engine databases.

They find the pages by following links in the pages they already have in their databases, but also rely on indexing web pages submitted by contributors.

The software 'crawls' through the web pages using elements such as titles, content, HTML tags etc. to build tables linking pages and their keywords.

The pages stored in the search-engine database can then be searched by keyword.

Bot

The term **bot** comes from the word **robot**. The term is used because it describes software that performs an automated task over the internet that would be time-consuming, repetitive or impossible for a human to perform.

A search-engine **spider** is just one example of a bot. Bots are also used in e-commerce to gather information on products for sale and to find the website with the best price.

Another example of the use of bots is chatrooms, where bots can be used to greet people when they enter a chatroom and can analyse the dialogue to kick people out if they violate the chatroom rules.

 DON'T FORGET

Crawlers are also commonly known as spiders, since they crawl like a spider around the web looking for websites to index in databases.

 **ONLINE**

Web crawlers are governed by policies that restrict their behaviour. Use a search engine to investigate the 'politeness policy' for a search engine such as Google.

 THINGS TO DO AND THINK ABOUT

One of the original chat bots is a program created in 1966 called Eliza.

Visit www.nlp-addiction.com/chatbot/eliza and have a conversation with Eliza.

 ONLINE TEST

How well have you learned this topic? Take the test at www.brightredbooks.net

TECHNICAL IMPLEMENTATION (REQUIREMENTS)

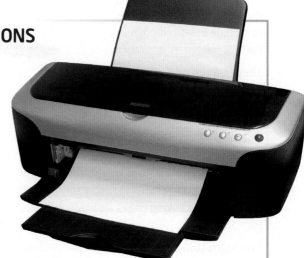

HARDWARE CONSIDERATIONS

Input and Output Devices

An information system requires input and output devices to enter and display data. Consideration must be taken of which type of devices are best suited to a specific type of system.

To enter a borrowed book's ISBN number, a large library would use a barcode scanner rather than a keyboard, which would be too slow.

The choice of printer used for printing a large commercial catalogue would be a colour laser printer, since it is faster and a higher resolution than an inkjet printer.

Processor Type, Speed (Hz) and Cores

The **processor** is responsible for executing the program and therefore must have a specification that meets the requirements of the software being run. There are many types of processors produced by different manufacturers, and the processor must be compatible with the hardware and the operating-system environment in which it will be used.

A high **clock speed** is required if the software is intensive on processor activity. Current clock speeds are typically in the range 4 GHz to 8 GHz.

Memory (RAM, ROM, Cache)

Very often, a program will run with the minimum amount of RAM – but it will run slowly, as parts of the program have to be loaded from the hard disc when required, which takes longer than accessing instructions directly from main memory.

Even if the operating system is disc-based, a computer needs at least a small amount of ROM to permanently store the bootstrap loader program which locates and loads the operating system.

Fast-access cache memory can improve the speed of execution of a program; so, the amount of cache is an important factor if performance is a key issue.

Device Type (Smartphone, Tablet, Laptop, Desktop, Supercomputer)

In general, the cost, processor speed and storage capacity of computing devices all increase in the order: smartphone, tablet, laptop, desktop, supercomputer.

A desktop or laptop computer would be preferred over a tablet or smartphone if a high performance is required or a large amount of data has to be keyed in, or if a large screen is required and portability is not an issue.

A supercomputer is an extremely expensive and powerful computer that would be used by large organisations in areas such as weather forecasting and simulation of real situations like global warming.

ONLINE

Head to www.brightredbooks.net to investigate clock speeds available on computing devices.

DON'T FORGET

More powerful systems may require a processor with more than one **core**. Dual- and quad-core processors are commonly used in high-resolution video games and video-editing.

DON'T FORGET

Portability is also an important factor when choosing a device to run an information system. A tablet or laptop would be selected rather than a desktop computer when the system has to be accessed from different locations.

SOFTWARE CONSIDERATIONS

Operating Systems

Software-development languages are used to create software that runs on specific operating-system platforms. A program written to run on the Windows 8 operating system will not run on the Mac OSX operating system. Operating systems are constantly being upgraded, therefore the version of the operating system being used can also affect compatibility.

Licensing

A software **licence** is the legal right to use a software package within the terms listed by the manufacturer of the software.

Many organisations require a **site licence** which allows them to run several copies of a software package. A site licence is an agreement with a software company to use a specified number of copies of a software package within a defined site such as a school or a business. Some site licences can be used for an unlimited number of users, while others restrict the number of users.

Proprietary vs Open Source

Proprietary software exists to make profits for the company that produced it – and the source code is usually a closely guarded secret.

Open source is software whose source code is available for free on the internet to the general public for use and/or to modify from its original design.

A well-known example of open-source software is the Linux operating system. Two examples of proprietary software are Apple's Mac OS and Microsoft Office.

Shown below is a table comparing open-source and proprietary software.

	Proprietary	Open source
Cost	The software costs money to buy.	Free to use and modify.
Support	Support is provided at a cost by the company that produced it.	Support is provided by a community of users and developers.
Modifications	Only the manufacturer can modify the source code.	Anyone can modify the source code.

Portability

The portability of software means how easily it can be adapted to run on a different system from the one that it was originally written for. For example, the Python programming language creates portable software, since the programs will run on Windows, Mac OS and Linux operating systems.

Another aspect of portability is how easily web pages can be transferred between different browsers. A web page that displays correctly in Internet Explorer may not display the same in Chrome.

Current Trends in Operating-system Design

The first operating systems, such as MS DOS in the early 1980s, used the keyboard to enter the user's commands. This has been almost totally replaced by graphical user interfaces, such as Windows and Mac OS, which use a mouse to point and select. Mobile operating systems such as iOS and Android have appeared in the last few years to run smartphone and tablet computers. Current desktop/laptop operating systems such as Windows 8 have touchscreen input but still retain the full functionality of a desktop computer operating system.

THINGS TO DO AND THINK ABOUT

Your school or college will use software from a variety of sources. Ask your teacher or network manager what open-source and proprietary software is used on the network and what licensing agreements are in place.

ONLINE TEST

Take the 'Technical Implementation' test at www.brightredbooks.net

TECHNICAL IMPLEMENTATION (STORAGE)

INTRODUCTION

An important part of implementing an information system is to select a suitable backing storage device to meet the requirements of the system by considering factors such as capacity, speed, compatibility, portability and so on.

Backing storage devices are used to permanently store program and data files in a computer system.

Some devices are built into the computer system, such as a hard disc drive. External devices are connected to the computer system through an interface (USB, FireWire etc.), such as an external hard disc drive.

STORAGE DEVICES

Backing storage devices can be classified as **magnetic**, **optical** or **solid-state** devices.

Magnetic

Magnetic devices store bits in two states of magnetisation on a specially coated surface. They include hard disc and magnetic tape.

Currently, hard-disc capacities are typically of the order of 1 terabyte. Magnetic tape capacities range from tens of gigabytes up to tens of terabytes.

Optical

Optical devices are so named because they use a laser to read and write data in the form of pits and lands on the surface of a disc. They include CD, DVD and Blu-ray discs. The first optical discs were CD-ROM (Read-Only Memory) discs, which could only be read from but not written to. Today, recordable CD-R, DVD-R and Blu-ray-R discs and rewriteable CD-RW, DVD-RW and Blu-ray-RE discs are commonly available. Typical capacities and data-transfer speeds of optical discs are shown in the table below.

Optical disc	CD	DVD	Blu-ray
Capacity	650 Mb	4·7 Gb	25 Gb
Data transfer speed (megabits per second)	7	33	72

Solid state

Solid-state storage devices have no moving parts but are made entirely of electronic components. They include memory cards (flash cards) used in digital cameras and USB memory sticks.

Memory sticks and memory cards typically have a capacity in the range 2 Gb to 256 Gb.

Flash memory can operate at read and write speeds of tens of megabits per second.

INTERFACE TYPE AND SPEED

The function of an interface is to connect a backing storage device or any other peripheral device to the CPU and to cope with differences in how the device and the CPU operate. There are different types of interfaces, each of which have different data transfer rates.

The table alongside gives some commonly used interfaces and their data transfer rates.

Interface	Transfer rate
FireWire	800 Mbps
USB 2.0	480 Mbps
USB 3.0	5 Gbps
Bluetooth 2.0	3 Mbps
Bluetooth 4.0	24 Mbps

ONLINE

Visit www.brightredbooks. net for further information on interfaces. Follow the link and enter terms such as 'FireWire', 'USB', 'Bluetooth' etc. into the site search box.

STORAGE AND BACKUP STRATEGIES

A system will require to store programs and data that are available 'live' for the daily operation of the system. It will also require offline storage for backups and the archiving of data.

Distributed storage is a term which describes the distribution of data on the file servers and computers connected to a network. It may also involve **cloud** storage systems to share the load.

Offline storage refers to discs, magnetic tapes, USB memory sticks etc. that are used to store data that is not connected to the system.

Backup Server

Some systems have a backup server that has the configuration and software of the network server in place so that it can replace it immediately in the event of failure.

RAID (Random Array of Inexpensive Discs)

A RAID system involves the server duplicating network data to a series of inexpensive discs. This allows the reinstallation of the data on a failed disc from the RAID discs to be done 'live' without the need to shut down the system.

Mirror Discs

This is the act of writing data to two discs simultaneously so that, in the event of failure of one disc, the other can be used instantly.

Tape

Backups used to be kept on magnetic tape because the tapes are cheap and portable.

Backup Schedule

Usually, a daily backup tape is rotated every 5 days, with an additional weekly backup rotated every 4 weeks so that data can be recovered up to a month ago.

CURRENT TRENDS IN STORAGE SYSTEMS

The amount of data in the world is growing at an increasing rate. It has been estimated that 90% of the data in the world today was created in the last two years. Consequently, storage systems have accelerated in their capacity and speed to cope with the large amounts of data being stored and accessed.

Trends include a rise in the amount of cloud storage space available to users, increasing capacity of backing storage devices and the development of high-speed interfaces.

 THINGS TO DO AND THINK ABOUT

Capacity, speed and cost should be considered when selecting a backing storage device for a computer system. It is important that you keep up with current prices and specifications of storage devices.

ONLINE TEST

Take the 'Technical Implementation' test online at www.brightredbooks.net

TECHNICAL IMPLEMENTATION (NETWORKING/CONNECTIVITY)

SERVER PROVISION AND CLOUD SYSTEMS

Server Provision

Server provision is the process of assigning storage space on the disc drive of a server computer on a network. Shared resources can be made available to network users by having shared access to files, individual folders and drives. Storing data on a server is restrictive in that data can only be accessed from a computer on the network, which is typically a small area such as an office or a school.

Cloud Systems

Cloud storage systems store data on a remote computer that is attached to the internet. This allows users to access their data anywhere in the world provided they have access to the internet. There is no specific data limit in cloud systems, but most companies will set a maximum which is less than 100 Gb.

Accessing data in the cloud depends on the speed of the internet connection, and it can be time-consuming to upload and download large amounts of data.

PUBLIC, PRIVATE AND HYBRID

Public Clouds

Public cloud storage is provided by a storage service provider that hosts and manages data storage publicly for many different users.

A public cloud offers cloud services which are effective for sharing resources, but it is not the most secure and reliable.

This is the best system in situations such as several people working in collaboration on a project and requiring the ability to add storage capacity at peak times.

Private Clouds

Private cloud storage is similar to public cloud storage in that it provides a similar management of data. However, private systems are not publicly accessible and are owned by a single organisation and by any authorised companies outside the organisation. Private clouds are appropriate for organisations that need a high level of security and customisation of their data.

This is the best system in situations which require strict security and data privacy and where the organisation is large enough to run a cloud data centre effectively on its own.

Hybrid Clouds

Hybrid cloud storage is a combination of the public and private cloud systems.

An organisation might use a public cloud for data where security is not an issue but use a private cloud for sensitive data such as customer details.

By using public storage for at least part of its data, a company can reduce its costs, since private storage is less cost-effective.

CLOUD-BASED SERVICES

These are services made available to users on the internet by a cloud computing provider as opposed to being provided from a company's own network servers.

Online data storage is an example of a cloud-based service. Gmail and Hotmail are cloud-based e-mail services which allow users to access their e-mail from any computing device with an internet connection. The e-mails, contacts and so on are hosted on Google's and Microsoft's servers rather than being stored locally on the user's computer.

Cloud computing is growing at a rapid rate, especially in areas of social networking (e.g. Facebook, Twitter, LinkedIn) and media services (e.g. YouTube, iTunes, Picasa).

There is an increasing trend for applications such as Microsoft Office, which have traditionally been installed and used on desktop/laptop computers, to be offered as a cloud-based service with Office Web Apps.

WEB HOSTING

Web hosting is a service that allows organisations and individuals to make their website accessible via the World-Wide Web.

Web hosts can also provide cloud storage by providing data-centre space. Many internet service providers (ISPs) offer web-hosting services free of charge to their customers, but the space is usually fairly limited. Personal web pages often only require a single web page; but a full-scale website, such as one used for e-commerce, may require a database to manage content and to install and run scripts to provide more complex functionality.

ONLINE

Open the home page of the ISP that you use at home and investigate the web-hosting services provided by this ISP.

CURRENT TRENDS IN NETWORKING AND CONNECTIVITY

With the increasing demand for portable devices such as mobile, tablet and laptop computers, there has been a consistent increase in the bandwidth of their connections. Media files such as images, music and video are large files, and the technology has advanced to allow the transmission of such files between devices.

4G (fourth generation) is the next upgrade in mobile network development, which provides users with much faster data transfer speeds than the existing 3G technology.

The data transfer rate for 3G is in the range 0·5 to 1·5 Mbps, whereas 4G offers 2 to 12 Mbps.

DON'T FORGET

Make sure that you thoroughly learn the terms and concepts covered in this book. In assessments, your answers need to include relevant technical terms and to be detailed and clear.

Transmission Media

Faster and more reliable transmission media are now available, such as optical fibres, and there is an increasing growth in the use of wireless connections, although it is relatively slow compared to cable connections.

Improved Hardware

Faster processors and higher-capacity main memory and backing stores have improved the performance of computer networks and therefore made them a more attractive proposition to organisations to deliver their IT requirements.

THINGS TO DO AND THINK ABOUT

Cloud services allow organisations and individuals to reduce the costs of investing in hardware and the installation of software on their devices. They also reduce maintenance costs, since the solutions are all web-based, and even older computers can be used to access cloud services. For these reasons, it is certain that cloud-based services will become increasingly widespread in the future.

ONLINE TEST

Take the 'Technical Implementation' test online at www.brightredbooks.net

SECURITY RISKS

VIDEO LINK

Watch the clip on phishing at www.brightredbooks.net

DON'T FORGET

Changing your password regularly is one way to guard against your password being used by someone who has obtained it using keylogger software.

VIDEO LINK

Learn more about denial of service by watching the clip at www.brightredbooks.net

DON'T FORGET

It is a common mistake to state that a DoS attack is brought about by flooding a server with a vast amount of data but not mentioning that it is in a short period of time. It is the fact that the server can't deal with a large volume of data in a short period of time that brings it down.

SPYWARE, PHISHING AND KEYLOGGING

Spyware

This is software that is used to capture information on your activities on a computer. Spyware can keep a record of which websites you have visited and can capture your e-mail messages, passwords, credit-card details and so on.

Phishing

Phishing is a scam to gather personal information from unsuspecting users by using a false website that has the appearance of a legitimate site. The false website can ask the user to enter details such as their name, address, phone number, social-security number and credit-card number.

There are several ways to identify counterfeit websites:

- Spelling and grammatical errors
- Poor-quality, unprofessional-looking graphics
- Poorly designed and laid-out website
- Addressing the user as 'customer' or 'client' instead of mentioning the user's name
- Asking you to send sensitive data such as your password or account details.

Keylogger

A keylogger is an item of software that logs a user's keystrokes and saves them to a file. The file can then be used to steal personal data including usernames, passwords and other private information. Keylogger programs can be identified and removed by anti-virus software.

ONLINE FRAUD AND IDENTITY THEFT

Online Fraud

This is any type of fraud scheme that uses the internet for theft. Examples are the non-delivery of paid-for goods, transactions carried out with stolen credit/debit cards, and bad-cheque scams. Criminals can obtain credit-card details by posing as a legitimate website and can then use the captured details to buy goods and services.

Identity Theft

Criminals can steal your identity by finding out your personal details on computer systems and then using this information to open bank accounts and obtain credit cards, loans and documents such as passports and driving licences in your name.

DENIAL-OF-SERVICE ATTACKS

A **denial-of-service attack** is when a network server, or a resource such as hard-disc space, is put under so much pressure that the network cannot provide its normal services to legitimate users.

DoS attacks involve bombarding the network with a high volume of data in a short period of time so that the network cannot cope, and its operations grind to a halt.

TYPES OF ATTACK

Bandwidth Consumption

This attack degrades the performance of a server by sending it a large number of data packets in a short period of time. For example, a **smurf attack** is mounted by sending a packet with a false source address to the broadcast address of a network. (Giving a packet a false source address is called **spoofing**.) The packet contains a **ping message**, which is a technique for checking that a communication link is working properly. All of the computers on the network then reply to the ping message, which is actually the address of the target server.

Resource Starvation

An attack can consume other resources apart from bandwidth in order to bring down a server.

For example, the server's hard-disc space can be used up by sending a large volume of e-mail messages.

Programming Flaw

Software is often released with flaws in the code. This type of attack exploits weaknesses in server software and operating systems.

Routing

This attack involves hi-jacking data packets and routing them to the target server, which then gets flooded with data packets, or redirecting packets to a false destination to deny legitimate requests.

Domain Name Service (DNS)

In this attack, a large number of DNS queries with a spoofed IP address of the target server are sent to a DNS server. The DNS server then floods the target server with an excessive number of replies.

REASONS FOR ATTACKS

There are several reasons why DoS attacks are carried out.

Malicious

Individuals think that it is good fun to bring down an organisation's network.

Personal

Disgruntled employees who bear a grudge can see a DoS attack as revenge against their employer.

Political

Sometimes, DoS attacks can be politically motivated, such as an attack on a government network or to bring down a rival company in business.

COSTS OF ATTACKS

A DoS attack can be very costly to an organisation – for several reasons:

1   The loss of business during the attack downtime

2   The cost of repair and response to the attack

3   Loss of confidence by users in the organisation

4   Disruption to the organisation.

VIDEO LINK

Head to www. brightredbooks.net to watch the clip on Botnets.

ONLINE

Head to www. brightredbooks.net to read more about anti-virus software.

 # THINGS TO DO AND THINK ABOUT

There have been many famous DoS attacks, ranging from political attacks on government networks to 'fun' attacks carried out by teenage boys.

Use the internet to investigate some famous DoS attacks.

ONLINE TEST

Test yourself on this topic online at www. brightredbooks.net

SECURITY PRECAUTIONS

Symmetric Encryption

Symmetric encryption is the simplest form of encryption. It encrypts data using a secret key and an encryption algorithm. Both the sender and the receiver need to have a copy of the secret key, which is kept secure.

The encryption algorithm processes the data with the secret key to produce **ciphertext**, which is transmitted over the insecure channel.

The receiver applies the secret key to the ciphertext using the decryption algorithm in order to retrieve the original data.

Symmetric encryption is simple and fast to implement, but it is difficult to manage the exchange of the secret key over an insecure channel.

Asymmetric Encryption

Asymmetric encryption is a more complex encryption method that uses a combination of a public and a private key to encrypt data.

If the public key is used to encrypt the message, then only the private key can be used with the decryption algorithm in order to retrieve the original data.

If the private key is used for encryption, then the resulting ciphertext can only be decrypted using that person's public key to ensure that the message is from who it claims to be from.

Asymmetric encryption is more complicated and slower to implement than symmetric encryption but is much more secure.

One of the benefits of asymmetric encryption is that the sender and the receiver do not need to exchange a private key first. The public key is available to anyone who needs to send an encrypted message to the receiver, but only the receiver can decrypt it because only the receiver has the private key.

DIGITAL CERTIFICATES AND SIGNATURES

Digital Signatures

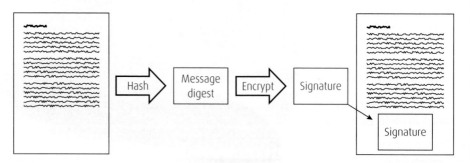

A **digital signature** is a piece of code that can be attached to a message which uniquely identifies the sender and therefore guarantees that the message is from the person it claims to be from. A digital signature can also be used to ensure that the message has not been altered.

The public and private key system can be used to create digital signatures. The private key can be used to attach a digital signature to data being transmitted. A **hashing algorithm** is applied to the data to be transmitted to create a unique **message digest**. This message digest is encrypted using the private key and is transmitted along with the data as a digital signature.

contd

ONLINE

Find out more about digital signatures on the website www.youdzone.com/signature.html

At the receiving end, the hashing algorithm is applied to the message to produce the message digest, and the attached signature is decrypted using the sender's public key to produce the original message digest. If the two message digests are identical, then the recipient knows that the signature is valid and that the data has not been tampered with in transit.

Digital Certificates

A **digital certificate** is an electronic 'passport' that allows a person, computer or organisation to communicate securely over the internet. A digital certificate is a package of information that identifies a user with information such as the user's name, the name of the organisation that issued the certificate (the Certificate Authority), the user's e-mail address and country and the user's public key.

The certificate authority acts as a middleman that both users trust. It confirms the identity of each user and provides the public keys of each user to the other.

When two users require a secure encrypted communication, one sends a query over the internet to the other user, who sends back a copy of the certificate. The other user's public key can be extracted from the certificate.

 VIDEO LINK

Watch an online tutorial on Digital Signatures at www.brightredbooks.net

SERVER-SIDE VALIDATION OF ONLINE FORM DATA

A website often requires the user to enter data into a form which is then submitted online. Examples of this would be booking a holiday, registering with an organisation, purchasing goods online and so on.

Server-side scripts are used to ensure that the data that has been entered into the form is valid. For example, the server-side script can give an error message if data has not been entered into essential fields such as a departure airport or the number of passengers. It can also perform more complex tasks such as checking that credit-card details are valid.

ON THE BOOK A FLIGHT FORM AT JETBLUE.COM...

...DEFAULTS ARE SET TO NO PASSENGERS.

IF UNCHANGED, THIS RESULTS IN AN ERROR.

BIOMETRICS IN INDUSTRY

Using **biometrics** for security is the science of identifying physical characteristics (fingerprints, eyes, hands) of a person using devices that include fingerprint readers and retinal scanners. Advantages of biometrics are: no need to remember passwords; faster entering of data; and forgery is almost impossible.

Some uses in industry include:
- Airports are increasingly using biometric technology to effectively identify passengers at border control using iris scans and fingerprinting.
- Some schools use biometric payment systems for students to pay for lunches. Instead of paying for lunch with cash, students are verified by their biometrics, and money is taken out of their account.
- The benefits include: removing the need to carry cash; students who lose money don't need to go without food; and queues are smaller.
- USB memory sticks are now readily available which use the owner's fingerprint to unlock the device.

 ONLINE

Read the article at www.brightredbooks.net to find out about current developments in biometric technology.

 ONLINE

Head to www.brightredbooks.net to read about the disadvantages of biometric technology.

 ## THINGS TO DO AND THINK ABOUT

Try to make up a list of the biometric scans that you have been personally exposed to in your life. Think about airport security, your school, visits to museums and so on.

 ONLINE TEST

How well have you learned this topic? Take the test at www.brightredbooks.net

LEGAL IMPLICATIONS

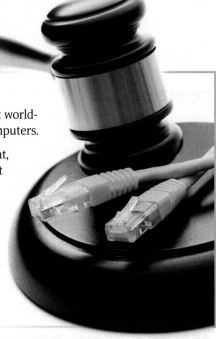

INTRODUCTION

There are several laws (applying in the UK but not world-wide) that have a direct bearing on the use of computers.

These are the Computer Misuse Act, the Copyright, Designs and Patents Act, the Communications Act and the Regulation of Investigatory Powers Act.

THE COMPUTER MISUSE ACT

This act is concerned with the misuse of computing technology to hack into confidential data and to purposely send destructive viruses to other people's computers.

Hacking into computer systems has been around as long as the internet. One of the problems with global communication is that it can be misused to gain access to confidential information to view it, change it or delete it. Before this act was introduced, there was no specific law that made these activities illegal.

The following activities are made illegal by the Computer Misuse Act:

- Gaining access to data held on a computer without permission, e.g. looking at someone else's files
- Gaining access to data held on a computer with the intention to commit a criminal offence, e.g. hacking into the bank's computer and wanting to increase the amount in your account
- Altering data held on a computer without permission, e.g. writing a virus to destroy someone else's data.

DON'T FORGET

You are not expected to become a lawyer during a computing course – but make sure that you know the main activities covered by the laws in this section.

THE COPYRIGHT, DESIGNS AND PATENTS ACT

This law protects authors of software, music, video etc. by ensuring that their work is not used without their permission.

- The creators have the right to control the ways in which their material may be used.
- Copying, editing and publishing another person's work must be done with their permission.
- It is illegal to copy/use computer programs without permission or a licence.
- Copying text or images from a web page is a breach of copyright.

Plagiarism

Plagiarism is passing off the ideas of another person as one's own without crediting the source. This has always been around, but clearly the abundance of electronic articles on the internet on any subject has made this crime much easier to commit. At a school level, plagiarism can often be detected by a sudden improvement in the level of language used by the student or by using a search engine to find the sources that the student has passed off as his or her own work. Computer software exists that can be used to detect plagiarism.

THE COMMUNICATIONS ACT

The Communications Act covers many different aspects of communications using e-mails, text messages, social-media sites and so on. The Office of Communications (Ofcom) is a government authority that was set up to regulate electronic communications as well as television and radio broadcasts in the UK. An important part of this legislation is to protect people from damaging communications and broadcasts which are easily made remotely with a mobile phone or on social-media sites.

Under this act, it is illegal to:

- Send by means of a public electronic communications network a message or other matter that is offensive, indecent or threatening;
- Post offensive information on social-media sites such as Twitter or Facebook;
- Send a message by means of a public electronic communications network that is known to be false;
- Use other people's broadband connections without their permission.

For example, using a mobile phone to send a hoax 999 call to emergency services is an offence under this act. Many people have also been prosecuted for posting offensive remarks on Facebook about the behaviour of celebrities.

THE REGULATION OF INVESTIGATORY POWERS ACT (2000)

When the internet first appeared in the workplace, some employees abused the facilities for their own personal use and to have fun at their employers' expense. The Regulation of Investigatory Powers Act (2000) was created to protect employers from loss of time and money through employees wasting time on the internet and on other technologies instead of doing their work.

Software is readily available which allows the monitoring of employees' use of e-mail and the internet. It is now possible to trace the activities and movements of individuals on the internet and to provide summary information. Some people are worried that employers can collect and use this information against individuals' rights to personal privacy.

The Regulation of Investigatory Powers Act (2000) gives employers the right to monitor e-mails and telephone calls of their employees to make sure that their activities are work-related.

Arguments **for** the Regulation of Investigatory Powers Act:

- Businesses should have the right to ensure that their facilities are not being abused.
- Companies need to have a means of identifying employees who are wasting time to the cost of the company.
- It is a government law and therefore needs no justification.

Arguments **against** the Regulation of Investigatory Powers Act:

- Users should have the right that personal e-mails should be kept private.
- Users should have the right that all their personal data is kept confidential.
- The act is in opposition to the principles of freedom of speech.

ONLINE

For more information on other laws that apply to the use of technology, follow the link at www.brightredbooks.net and look up the Data Protection Act and Health and Safety Legislation.

THINGS TO DO AND THINK ABOUT

Not all of the Higher course is about technical issues concerning hardware and software. You should also be able to argue for and against social issues such as the legislation covered in this section.

You should also be able to identify situations where these acts apply and their implications for society.

ONLINE TEST

Test yourself on this topic online at www.brightredbooks.net

ENVIRONMENTAL IMPLICATIONS

INTRODUCTION

The growth of computers and IT equipment has transformed our world – not without some serious consequences for the environment. 'Green' protesters are keen to point out negative impacts on the environment, such as the **carbon footprint** caused by the use of computers; but there are also many ways in which computing technology is a benefit for the environment.

This spread covers the positive and negative impacts of computing technology on our environment.

NEGATIVE ENVIRONMENTAL IMPACT

The manufacture, use and disposal of IT equipment all require the use of electricity.

Electricity is mainly produced in power stations by burning coal and oil. This process produces large amounts of the **greenhouse gas** carbon dioxide as a by-product. Most scientists agree that this is a major factor in global warming and climate change.

Manufacture

The lifetime carbon footprint begins with digging up the raw materials out of the ground, which requires powering machinery and tools and transporting the materials to the next stage of processing.

The manufacture of computers in factories also requires electricity and further transport for distribution to the companies that sell them.

Computer Use

The largest carbon footprint comes from the use of computers, which obviously consume electricity on a daily basis.

Electricity consumption can be reduced by switching off equipment when it is not being used, such as printers, scanners and so on. Screensavers may have been very popular in the past, but they don't save energy. Leaving a computer in stand-by mode uses up much less energy.

Power-saving strategies can also help, such as turning off the computer and monitor when they are not being used. Use the **power down** settings on the computer to automatically shut down the computer when it is not being used for a lengthy period of time. Leaving a computer monitor on stand-by overnight produces enough energy to microwave 6 dinners!

In the UK, it is estimated that 66,000 homes could be powered by the energy wasted annually – which is equivalent to the output of 2 power stations.

Disposal

Computers contain poisonous chemicals such as mercury, lead and cadmium. Discarding outdated computing hardware improperly has consequences for pollution of the environment and contamination of water and air.

In the UK alone, more than 1 million tons of electronic equipment is disposed of each year. The Waste Electrical and Electronic Equipment Regulations 2006 were introduced to regulate the disposal of equipment by households and businesses. This regulation governs the safe disposal and recycling of computers and related devices.

Disposal of IT equipment also has a carbon footprint, since the hardware has to be transported to a dump, and machinery may be used to crush or process it.

contd

DON'T FORGET

The 'carbon footprint' of computing equipment and other electrical goods is a measure of how much carbon dioxide is produced in their lifetime.

ONLINE

Check out the article 'Computers should be greener' at www.brightredbooks.net

ONLINE

Read more about the environmental impact of computers at www.brightredbooks.net

Recycling instead of disposal is one answer to this problem. Computers whose performance becomes outdated could be upgraded with better processors and more memory instead of being discarded for new ones. On average, there are 11 ink cartridges thrown away every minute across the globe – and each will take between 400 and 1,000 years to decompose. Ink cartridges can be refilled for a fraction of the cost of buying a new one, which would help to reduce unnecessary waste.

There is also the issue of the **security of data** on discarded computers. Deleting a file from the hard disc removes it from the **directory**, but it can still be retrieved from the hard disc with utility software.

Special software that wipes the hard drive, or physically destroying the disc, are solutions to this problem.

POSITIVE ENVIRONMENTAL IMPACT

Paperless Office

To some extent, it could be argued that computers increase the amount of paper documents in circulation. However, they provide paperless communications, such as e-mail and online bill-paying, which play a big part in reducing the amount of trees cut down.

Downloading

Up until fairly recently, music, films and books were bought as physical products from shops. Today, a large and increasing percentage of these items is downloaded from websites and played or viewed on computing equipment without the need to manufacture books or DVDs. Even photographs taken by a digital camera can be loaded onto a digital photo frame without ever having a life on photographic paper.

Working from Home

Communication technology allows people doing certain types of job to work from home. For example, an advertising contractor who uses e-mail and telephone calls to contact clients can easily work from home rather than travelling to an office. This will save on the carbon footprint caused by travelling to work and will reduce the need for furnished office spaces.

Efficiency

Systems that use energy can be controlled better by computers and can save energy by making them more efficient in the consumption of energy. For example, central-heating systems automatically switch radiators off when the temperature reaches a desired level and switch the heating on only at the times of day when it is required.

Computer software is also used to monitor power use and to study our environment to better understand how it works and the impact of our actions on it.

 THINGS TO DO AND THINK ABOUT

Tablet computers have a smaller carbon footprint than laptops, which in turn have less impact than desktop computers.

 ONLINE TEST

Head to www. brightredbooks.net and take the test on environmental implications.

ECONOMIC IMPACT

E-COMMERCE

The internet has transformed the way in which people buy and sell goods. The attractions to consumers include that prices can be compared to get the best deal, shopping can be carried out at any time, and money is saved on travelling to shops.

Internet sales in the UK alone amount to several hundred billion pounds a year and are still growing.

Studies have estimated that 40% of shops will have to shut in the next five years as customers turn their backs on traditional stores in favour of online shopping.

E-commerce gives the seller several advantages over traditional high-street shops to sell goods:

1 There is no need for the expense of buying/renting high-street shops and paying for furnishings and staff.

2 The cost of goods can be reduced, since there are fewer overheads, and prices will be competitive.

3 There are no 'middlemen' to take some of the profit, since retailers deal directly with the customers.

4 EFT (Electronic Funds Transfer) reduces the security problems in handling cash.

MAINTAINABILITY

All online information systems will require maintenance from time to time to modify the existing system to respond to changes in the needs of the business and the consumers. For example, an online company selling dolls may wish to modify its website to add and remove products, provide 3-D views of its dolls or simply to improve the website's appearance. Companies will usually need to take their site offline while they perform maintenance on the website. It is important that sales are interrupted for as little time as possible so as not to have too big an impact on profits while the maintenance takes place. Big companies may use backup servers to keep the old site available to customers until the new site is ready to become live.

Businesses will attempt to cause as little disruption to their customers as possible by carrying out maintenance when they expect their site activity to be low and limiting the downtime to 1 or 2 hours. Also, they will often give advance warning of dates and times when the site will be down.

Example:

This was a notification from eBay concerning maintenance of its website:

The eBay system will be undergoing general maintenance from approximately 23:00 PT on Thursday, October 2nd to 01:00 PT on Friday, October 3rd.

During this maintenance period, certain eBay site features may be intermittently unavailable or slow.

In addition, PayPal will be performing maintenance on their systems on October 2nd as well. From approximately 23:00 PT to midnight, some PayPal services may be unavailable.

SCALABILITY

Scalability is a measure of how well a business information system can cope with increasing demand as the business grows. It is essentially a term that describes the potential for economic growth within a company. A company that scales up well is able to maintain or even increase its profitability when tested by increased demands.

For example, if a company that sells dolls over the internet suddenly receives a series of large orders, it is faced with important decisions about growth and its costs. To meet the orders, it will need to take on more staff and machinery, and it might need to buy or rent larger premises. The company can't be sure whether the increased demand will continue or whether it is just a blip in sales.

On the other hand, a company that sells items of software by downloading it to customers over the internet does not face the same issues of scalability. Although the cost of software development is high, there is very little cost associated with actually delivering the software. The company could gain a million customers overnight, but its cost of delivering products to these customers won't increase.

Because there is little delivery cost per customer associated with digital downloads, creating a product that can be sold and then downloaded online is a very scalable business idea. In addition to software, businesses can create e-books, music, games, videos and templates for presentations or documents that can be downloaded after a customer purchases them online.

 THINGS TO DO AND THINK ABOUT

Consider any goods or services that you have purchased over the Internet. Try to list any benefits or problems this caused compared to making traditional purchases in shops.

 ONLINE TEST

How well have you learned this topic? Test yourself online at www.brightredbooks.net

SOCIAL IMPACT

CENSORSHIP AND FREEDOM OF SPEECH

Internet censorship in the United Kingdom involves various measures including filtering internet sites based on their content, and laws that make the publication or possession of certain material illegal.

Firewalls can be used to block certain sites; and governments are taking steps to introduce a broad system of default blocking of certain types of content to all internet users in the UK.

Some people believe that censorship is a violation of people's rights to freedom of speech. There are no government restrictions on access to the internet, but it is not the case that anyone can post anything over the internet. For example, copyright law has been used to shut down websites that allow file-sharing.

Laws against libel (written smearing of someone's character) apply equally to the internet as to any other media.

Over the last few years, there has been an increase in surveillance of internet activity by state agencies to fight against terrorism and crime and to protect children.

The law provides for freedom of speech and does not allow interference with private individual communications.

PRIVACY AND ENCRYPTION

In the modern technological world, there are many ways in which the privacy of people is threatened. Companies can monitor the internet sites people visit, and then the information can be used to send advertisements based on the browsing history. Personal information can be made available on social-media websites; and bank and credit-card details are sent to various websites to purchase goods. Browsing logs, search queries and Facebook profiles can all be automatically processed to gather confidential details about an individual, such as political and religious views, addresses, telephone numbers, race and so on.

Cookies

A **cookie** stores data on a user's computer to remember the user's activities when visiting a website.

For example, cookies can store a username and password so that you do not have to sign in every time you return to a website. A cookie can also track your preferences and show you other websites that might be of interest to you.

Some of the benefits of cookies are also seen as negative. For example, one of the most common ways of online theft is by hackers taking confidential information such as usernames and passwords that a cookie saves.

The browsing habits and frequently visited websites which are saved in cookies can be sold to other companies, who can then flood the user with unwanted junk e-mail.

Encryption

Encryption is used to make data such as electronic transactions and online payments confidential and secure by scrambling numbers, text, sounds and images. If the encrypted data is intercepted, then it can't be interpreted without the key to decrypt the data. There are various methods of encryption, but they all involve some form of mathematical transformation of data.

ONLINE

Go to www.brightredbooks.net and read several articles about censorship online.

DON'T FORGET

Most social-networking sites have settings to protect the personal information of their users. For example, for Facebook users, privacy settings are available to block certain individuals from seeing their profile; they can choose their 'friends'; and they can limit who has access to pictures and videos.

ONLINE

Open your browser and investigate the settings for Cookies and History. They will probably be on a Tools menu under Privacy or Security.

DON'T FORGET

Web browsers have settings that allow cookies to be deleted and blocked. This removes the privacy threat but may have an impact on the functionality of many websites.

GLOBAL CITIZENSHIP

Global Citizens

Only a couple of centuries ago, the majority of people in the world spent their entire lives in the community that they were born into. Most people spent their lives without travelling more than 100 miles from the place where they were born. The invention of trains and then aircraft allowed people to travel further and further afield and to meet other people in other communities and nations. In the current world, the internet has allowed people who may live on different sides of the planet to communicate in online communities. In a sense, people are becoming **global citizens** in that they can connect across national boundaries and are citizens of the world. This global communication has led to an increased awareness and sharing of other cultures and attitudes.

ONLINE COMMUNITIES

An **online community** is a virtual community that exists online whose members connect, provide resources and discuss issues to share a common interest.

An online community can take the form of an information system where anyone can post content, such as a bulletin-board system, or one where only a restricted number of people can place posts, such as web logs. Many online communities exist in social-media software such as Facebook, Twitter, chatrooms and forums that use voice, video text or avatars. Online communities have also become an extra means of communication between people who already know each other in real life.

 THINGS TO DO AND THINK ABOUT

More and more people are communicating by using technology across the globe without ever having physically met. This has an enormous impact on society and is making us more aware of other cultures in a way that was unimaginable only decades ago.

 ONLINE TEST

Test yourself on this topic online at www. brightredbooks.net

OUTCOMES AND UNIT ASSESSMENT

INTRODUCTION

Each of the two mandatory units (Software Design and Development; Information System Design and Development) requires you to achieve an assessment standard in a set of **learning outcomes**.

In the Information System Design and Development unit, there are **two** learning outcomes:

OUTCOMES

Outcome 1

Develop one or more information systems, using appropriate development tools such as databases or websites.

Outcome 2

Consider the factors involved in the design and implementation of an information system.

DETAILS OF THE OUTCOMES

Each of the two learning outcomes has several parts. All of the subsections must be achieved to gain a pass for the outcome.

Outcome 1

This is a practical outcome in which you have to achieve each of the following criteria though the development of information systems using appropriate development tools.

There are seven subsections to this outcome:

1.1 Applying contemporary design and development methodologies
1.2 Creating a complex structure with links
1.3 Incorporating good user interface design
1.4 Writing code
1.5 Integrating different media types
1.6 Identifying and rectifying errors
1.7 Testing against appropriate criteria.

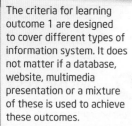

DON'T FORGET

The criteria for learning outcome 1 are designed to cover different types of information system. It does not matter if a database, website, multimedia presentation or a mixture of these is used to achieve these outcomes.

contd

Evidence for the design of the information system can be submitted in hard copy or electronically.

A structured chart can be used to show the overall plan and the user interface design in the form of wireframes, manual drawings/sketches and so on.

The links could be relationships between tables in a database or hyperlinks in a website.

The interface should be clear and well laid out and must also reflect the age or ability of the target audience.

Writing code can be achieved by using a scripting language such as JavaScript in a website or SQL (Structured Query Language) in a database.

You must integrate different media types into the information system such as text, graphic, sound and/or video.

You must identify and rectify errors as required and provide evidence of testing as the information system is developed. This can be done with appropriate printouts or by observation and conversation with your assessor.

You must provide a test plan with criteria for final testing of the information system, and then provide hard copy or electronic evidence of final test results.

Outcome 2

This is a written outcome in which you have to describe in detail several factors involved in the design and implementation of an information system.

Your teacher may not ask you to submit a written report. You may be asked to use a presentation package to present your results or to demonstrate your understanding by being orally questioned.

There are six subsections to this outcome:

2.1　Functionality, range and types of users
2.2　Technical implementation (hardware and software requirements)
2.3　Technical implementation (storage and connectivity)
2.4　Security risks and precautions
2.5　Legal and environmental implications
2.6　Economic and social impact.

The content of this book covers in general the topics addressed in this outcome. You should consult the relevant spreads as you carry out this task to focus on the key points. However, your report must address these issues in the context of the information system detailed in your assessment task.

DON'T FORGET

Make sure that your report on the design and development of an information system is placed in the context of the information system specified in your assessment. It is a common mistake to be too general and not to report in the context of a specific information system.

EVIDENCE

The evidence for Outcome 1 may be obtained from a single information system such as a database, a website or a multimedia application (or a mixture of these). Alternatively, the evidence may be obtained from a series of shorter tasks that involve the development of one or more types of information system.

The report for Outcome 2 should be in a form that can be presented to others (this does not need to be written but may be reported in some other format such as a presentation or a website).

 THINGS TO DO AND THINK ABOUT

You must achieve the learning outcomes for the unit assessments by yourself. However, you should take opportunities to seek advice from your teacher on how to proceed with the assessment tasks. Never expect the teacher to complete a task for you; but you can certainly ask for guidance and feedback on your progress.

REVISION QUESTIONS 1

QUESTION 1

Maggie is interested in birdwatching and has created her own website that includes images of birds, videos of bird behaviour and audio clips of birdsongs. She uses digital sound-editing software to edit the clips which will be imported into her website.

(a) One of the audio clips for an osprey lasts for 40 seconds. It is sampled at 24 kHz with a sample depth of 16 bits in stereo.

Calculate the filesize of this audio clip in an appropriate unit.

(b) Maggie uses the sound-editing software to reduce the size of the audio files.

State two methods of reducing the files' sizes without shortening their length.

(c) Video files can be reduced in size by applying compression techniques. Some file formats for video use lossy compression techniques, while others use lossless compression techniques.

(i) What is the difference between lossy and lossless compression?

(ii) Describe what is meant by interframe compression.

(iii) Give two techniques other than compression for reducing the size of video files.

(d) The video clips all last for 18 seconds and were captured at 25 frames per second with a resolution of 640 x 480 and 24-bit colour.

Calculate the size of one video file.

DON'T FORGET

This is a technical course, and you are expected to know the expansion of technical acronyms used in questions, such as RAM, CSS, ALU and so on.

QUESTION 2

Harry uses a digital camera to take the picture of his pet cat shown here. The image is then imported into a painting package, where it is saved in 24-bit colour with a resolution of 1,200 dpi.

ONLINE

Head to www. brightredbooks.net to see the answers to the questions from pp88–91.

(a) Harry compresses the image before sending it over the internet to friends around the world.

Why would RLE and LZW not have much effect on reducing the size of this image?

(b) Harry saves the image in the JPEG file format but notices a loss in the quality of the image.

Explain why the image is reduced in quality when saved as a JPEG file.

(c) Explain why GIF is a suitable file format for storing cartoon-style images but not images captured by a digital camera, such as the cat.

QUESTION 3

Toni Tortiglioni has a business that makes pasta in dozens of attractive shapes. He sells his products on a website and keeps the stock in his own warehouse.

(a) The website uses server-side scripts and client-side scripts to perform various functions.

State whether each of the following is carried out by a server-side or a client-side script, and explain your answer.

(i) Displaying a count of the number of 'hits' for the website.

(ii) The user clicking on a check box next to an image of a type of pasta in order to buy it.

(b) Before Toni started his website on the internet, he sold his pasta in several high-street shops.

Describe **two** advantages to Toni of using e-commerce instead of traditional shops to sell his products.

(c) Toni hired a website designer to create his website.

The designer used a website-authoring package, which he installed on Toni's computer.

Describe **one** compatibility issue that can arise when installing software.

QUESTION 4

Gwen is a student at a veterinary college. When she goes to the cafeteria for lunch, her fingerprint is read by a machine that deducts her purchase from her account.

(a) (i) What is the advantage of using fingerprint recognition in this situation?

(ii) Why might some people be concerned that the college is gathering fingerprint data on students?

(b) On a Wednesday afternoon, Gwen goes to the college library to do research on veterinary websites.

She has poor eyesight and usually develops a headache by the time she has finished.

What steps can the creators of the website take to improve the accessibility of their site for people with poor eyesight?

(c) Last term, Gwen had to write an essay on infectious diseases in badgers for a course assessment. One of the students in her class was accused of plagiarism.

Explain why plagiarism is an increasing problem in today's society.

(d) Sometimes, Gwen has to hand in printouts of her work to her tutor. She would prefer to submit the work in electronic form to reduce the carbon footprint.

Describe the lifetime carbon footprint of a printer in terms of manufacture, use and disposal.

 **DON'T FORGET**

When answering questions, it is important to read the information at the start of the question. This will often give a context and provide important details that will affect your answer.

 THINGS TO DO AND THINK ABOUT

It might seem an obvious thing to say – but read questions carefully. Every word can have a bearing on the answer. If you rush and skim, you might answer your own question and not the question in front of you.

REVISION QUESTIONS 2

QUESTION 1

Polar Pods is a company that makes miniature fridges. They are developing a website where users can create an account and purchase products.

Polar Pods would like to maximise the visits to their website by ensuring that the HTML code for the site is optimised for indexing by crawler software.

(a) Describe the purpose of crawler software.

(b) Give **two** ways in which the site can be optimised for indexing by crawler software.

(c) When users create an account, they can submit an online form containing their billing address and credit-card details for payment.

Why should Polar Pods make use of server-side validation as opposed to client-side validation of the online form data?

QUESTION 2

Hollywood Distribution Incorporated is a film company that manages the marketing of international films.

The company has a database to store details of films, actors, their agents and the film studio that made the film. The data is stored in the following four tables.

Actor	Agent	Film	Studio
Actor ID	Agent ID	Film ID	Studio ID
Actor name	Agent name	Actor ID	Studio name
Actor sex (M/F)	Agent sex (M/F)	Studio ID	Studio address
Actor date of birth	Agent telephone number	Budget	Contact name
Actor age	Agent address	Release date	Contact telephone number
Actor telephone number	Agent photo	Box-office takings	
Actor address			
Actor photo			
Agent ID			

(a) State **two** one-to-many relationships that exist between the tables.

The following form is used to enter each actor's details.

Actor	
Actor ID	666
Actor name	Brad Cruise
Actor sex (M/F)	M
Actor date of birth	010489
Actor telephone number	02734 596160
Actor address	5 Celluloid Drive
Actor photo	
Agent ID	123

(b) (i) Describe **two** ways in which the entering of data can be made more usable.

(ii) Explain why the actor's age is not included in the entry form.

(c) A film director requires information on the actors who have appeared in films made by the '3D Flicks' studio.

The following report is produced for the studio.

Describe in detail how the database software can be used to produce this report.

contd

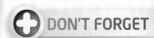
Studio: 3D Flicks				
Actor name	Gary Hammond	Sophie Rosebowl	Harry Ham	Amanda Wood
Actor photo				
Actor age	45	24	75	32
Agent telephone number	05533 410234	05533 808923	08997 435208	0667 550302

(d) The company is expanding to meet extra demand.

How easy will it be for the company to scale up the database to meet the new demands?

QUESTION 3

ShareView is a financial company which provides international stock-market values and share prices and allows visitors who have an account to buy and sell shares. It uses a dynamic database-driven website to display the rise and fall of the markets and the price of individual shares. Details of the markets and shares are held within a database.

(a) Describe two reasons why a dynamic database-driven website is a benefit for the users.

(b) The appearance of the text throughout all the web pages is managed using cascading style sheets (CSS).

Text	Font	Size	Colour	Style
Headings	Cambria	24	Black	Bold
Subheadings	Comic Sans MS	18	Red	Underline
Body text	Arial	12	Blue	Regular

Create a CSS rule that will implement the text formatting for the subheadings.

(c) Some users of the site have complained that the website can take a long time to download.

Describe how compression can be used to reduce the time to retrieve and display a web page.

QUESTION 4

Samantha and Lucy work for a fashion company called Teen Tiaras.

Most of the time, they work in partnership on graphic-design documents in a shared folder on the company's computer network. Some days, they work from home, but they still need to access the graphic files.

(a) Explain why cloud storage might be best suited to this situation.

(b) (i) Explain the difference between private cloud storage systems and public cloud storage systems.

(ii) Explain why Teen Tiaras might wish to use a hybrid cloud storage system.

 THINGS TO DO AND THINK ABOUT

Don't start your answer to a question by just repeating the question.

Example:

Question

What is the difference between private and public cloud storage systems?

Answer

The difference between private and public cloud storage systems is ...

This is not necessary, and indeed is a waste of valuable time in assessment conditions. A suitable answer to this question might start with: 'Public cloud storage systems host and manage data storage which is available to the public for many different users, whereas private ...'.

COURSE ASSESSMENT VALUE-ADDED UNIT

THE EXAM

INTRODUCTION

> **Course Assessment Structure**
> Component 1   Exam Paper: 90 marks
> Component 2   Assignment: 60 marks
> **Total:**   **150 marks**

The value-added unit is used to assess your attainment and to provide an overall grade for the course. The course assessment consists of an exam paper and a practical assignment. The exam is allocated 90 marks out of a total of 150 for the course assessment. Therefore the exam makes up 60% of the total marks for this course. The exam covers the content of the two mandatory units: Software Design and Development, and Information System Design and Development.

The question is set and marked by the SQA and is sat in centres under the exam conditions specified by the SQA.

ONLINE

The SQA exams start in April and continue through to the beginning of June. Months before the exams start, the exam timetable is published on the SQA website, where you can download your own personalised exam timetable.

THE EXAM PAPER

The exam paper has approximately 50% of the marks on each of the two mandatory units.

There are two sections in the exam paper.

Section 1: 20 marks

This section has short-answer questions that test your knowledge and understanding of the topics listed in the syllabus for each of the mandatory units.

Section 2: 70 marks

DON'T FORGET

Curriculum for Excellence has been developed to create **independent learners**. Be prepared for an exam that tests your problem-solving abilities and not simply the ability to memorise and regurgitate facts.

contd

This section has extended-response questions that test your ability to apply your knowledge and understanding in a challenging problem-solving context.

Total: 90 marks

The time allocation for the exam is two hours.

The exam has 90 marks that have to be gained in two hours. Allowing half an hour for reading and checking, you have on average 1 minute to obtain each mark. Use this to pace yourself. You want to strike a balance between finishing the exam too quickly and running out of time halfway through the paper. Finishing the exam far too early usually means that you have not given fully explained and detailed answers. You should be finishing Section 1 in around 25 minutes. It is also a good idea to leave yourself a few minutes the end of the exam to check over your answers.

PREPARATION

At the time of writing, there had not yet been a sitting of the exam for the new Higher. However, there is a specimen paper available which gives an indication of the level of difficulty and style of question that you can expect in the actual exam. Your teacher should be able to give you a copy of this paper; or you can download it from the SQA website. It is good preparation to work through this paper, as it will give you a feel for the exam. It is also a good idea to look at the marking scheme, where you will find worked answers that will give you an indication of the content and the detail that are expected in your answers.

There are companies that create imitation exam papers in the same structure and style as the official SQA exams. These are a useful source of revision for your exam. Don't worry if a few of the questions are 'over the top' in terms of level of difficulty or appear to be outside the course syllabus. This is simply because they are not official papers and have not been thoroughly checked in the same way as an SQA exam. Ask your teacher where you can obtain imitation exam papers, or to clarify any points about their questions.

You should see this book as an excellent way of consolidating the theory topics covered in class. If you thoroughly learn the content of this book, then you will have a strong foundation from which to tackle the exam. Remember that you can also use the online Bright Red Digital Zone for extra preparation. Your teacher is also a valuable resource for guidance and preparation. He/she can be a source of extra questions and revision materials, or can at least provide information on where to find them for yourself.

 THINGS TO DO AND THINK ABOUT

Each year, the SQA produces an examiner's report, which can be found on the SQA website. This report gives helpful comments on strong and weak areas of student performance and cut-off scores for each grade. This report can give you a useful insight into the exam process.

THE COURSEWORK TASK

INTRODUCTION

Course Assessment Structure	
Component 1	Exam Paper: 90 marks
Component 2	Assignment: 60 marks
Total:	**150 marks**

The practical assignment is allocated 60 marks out of a total of 150 for the course assessment. Therefore the practical coursework makes up 40% of the total marks for this course, and a good mark in this component can go a long way towards overall success.

THE ASSIGNMENT

You will be given an assignment chosen from a bank of assignments provided by the SQA. Your teacher will choose an assignment that is best suited to your skills and ability.

The purpose of the assignment is to assess your ability to produce a solution to an appropriate computing problem that is based upon the knowledge and skills that you have developed in the two mandatory units. It is set by the SQA and carried out under controlled conditions. This is an open-book assessment, which means that you can look over programs and information systems that you have previously written to refresh your memory on particular skills that you may have forgotten. You can use manuals and textbooks to get more information and extend your skills.

Your teacher is allowed to give you some hints and advice – but do not expect him/her to do the assignment for you. You are expected to show your own initiative in this task and to persevere with a problem in the search for a solution. If your teacher gives you significant support with a particular stage of the problem, then he/she will deduct marks for that stage.

Your teacher will know your strengths and weaknesses and will give you suitable preparation exercises to practise the required skills for the assignment.

The assignment is not just about finding a practical solution at the computer. It involves analysing a problem, the design of a solution, implementing the solution and then testing the solution. The necessary skills to address these stages should have been covered in your unit assessments and are described in the topics in this book. The assignment is broken down into a series of short tasks which guide you in clear stages through the assessment.

THE REPORT

A word-processed report on the analysis, design, implementation and testing must be provided. Make sure that the report is clear, well presented and free from silly mistakes and spelling and grammatical errors. Have a cover page and appropriate heading and subheading with consistency in the formatting. Page numbers and headers should be inserted, as should an index page. Avoid using multiple fonts and styles, which would make the document appear cluttered and too 'busy'.

People are impressed by appearances, so don't let your good practical work down by handing in a messy report that is difficult to read.

ONLINE

You can find lots more details of course assessment for the Higher course on the Scottish Qualifications Authority website at www.sqa.org.uk/sqa/56924.html

DON'T FORGET

The assignment will ask you to produce a program and an information system, such as a relational database or a complex website running scripts. It is very likely that the program will involve implementing one or more of the standard algorithms covered in the Algorithm Specification spread.

MARKS

The marks are allocated to the stages of your solution as shown below.

Analysing the problem	10 marks
Designing a solution	10 marks
Implementing a solution	20 marks
Testing the solution	10 marks
Reporting on the solution	10 marks

Evidence Checklist

Higher Computer Science Assignment

Progress Diary

Name: *Penelope Wilde*

Date	Notes of work done and changes made

Check the list below to make sure that you have completed all of the required stages and have collected all of the required evidence:

1   A record of progress through the assignment.
    This can be in the form of a log giving dates and the tasks completed.

2   A complete specification for the solution.

3   A design of the solution to the information system including the interface.

4   A design of the solution to the program including the interface.

5   Printouts of the information system.
    For example populated database tables, results of queries, webpages, etc.

6   A listing of the final program including internal commentary.

7   A test plan with evidence of testing.

8   The report including an evaluation of the solution.

THINGS TO DO AND THINK ABOUT

It cannot be overstressed that the software solutions for the assignment only make up one third of the marks. Make sure that you carefully read every word of the assignment and meet all of the requirements of the documentation write-up for analysis, design, testing and reporting to gain your best possible mark.